When Honour's at the Stake

WHEN HONOUR'S AT THE STAKE

Ideas of honour in Shakespeare's plays
by Norman Council

BOOKS
10 East 53d St., New York 10022
(a division of Harper & Row Publishers, Inc.)

Published in the U.S.A. 1973 by
HARPER & ROW PUBLISHERS, INC.
BARNES & NOBLE IMPORT DIVISION

ISBN 06-4912922

Printed in Great Britain

For Cathy

Contents

Contents

Chapter 1

Ideas of Honour in Shakespeare's England

In the scene in *3 Henry VI* which displays Margaret's and Warwick's rival entreaties for support from the King of France, Shakespeare has King Lewis ask Warwick 'upon [his] conscience' if Yorkist Edward be the true and rightful King of England. Warwick, who has consistently supported the Yorkist cause and branded Henry a usurper, assures Lewis, with a compelling oath, of Edward's legitimate claim.

> Thereon I pawn my credit and mine honour.
>
> (III. iii. 116)[1]

King Lewis is by this and other assurances convinced, and by affiancing his sister-in-law, the Lady Bona, to Edward he concurs in the plan to ally France with the Yorkist crown. Some sixty lines in the scene after Warwick has thus pawned his honour on Edward's legitimate claim, messengers arrive to announce the contrary marriage of Edward and the Lady Grey. This marriage, as the play introduces it, is irrelevant to the legitimacy of Edward's claim to the throne, but it is an affront to Warwick, for it betrays his embassy to treat of marriage in the French court. Shakespeare has Warwick repudiate Edward in terms which make it clear that Edward's supposed right to the throne has considerably less sway over Warwick than do the demands of his affronted honour.

> No more my king, for he dishonours me,
> But most himself, if he could see his shame.
>
> (III. iii. 184–5)

Warwick lists the earlier injuries he now sees himself to have suffered in Edward's service, then, again, justifies his change in allegiance by appealing to honour.

> And am I guerdon'd at the last with shame?
> Shame on himself! for my desert is honour;

11

And to repair my honour, lost for him,
I here renounce him and return to Henry.

(III. iii. 191–4)

The speeches Shakespeare gives Warwick here mirror the most widespread definition of honour in sixteenth-century England; honour is
the reward due to virtuous action. Warwick's complaint that he is
'guerdon'd' with shame although his 'desert' is honour reflects this
basic definition, just as his repudiation of Edward for honour's sake
reflects the ironic and contradictory consequences of its pervasive
influence.

On another occasion, at the moment when Henry is forced to recognize York and his sons as heirs to the crown, Shakespeare also defines
the characters as being primarily committed to the principles of honour.
The first scene of the play enlists Northumberland, Clifford, and
Westmoreland on Henry's Lancastrian side, but when Henry quails
before Warwick's show of force, these allies desert him. Warwick's
threat to 'write up [York's] title with usurping [i.e., Henry's] blood'
(I. i. 169) makes the nature of Henry's choice clear; his failure to risk
his life for honour's sake alienates his sometime allies. They will
regroup around the warlike Margaret and her ambitious son, but in
this first scene the legitimacy of Henry's claim is as secondary for them
as that of Edward's will later be for Warwick. All three allies merely
assume that Henry should have chosen death before dishonour. Westmoreland's parting line describes Henry as a 'faint-hearted and
degenerate king,/ In whose cold blood no spark of honour bides'
(I. i. 183–4). Northumberland calls Henry's an 'unmanly deed'
(I. i. 186). Clifford wants him 'abandon'd and despis'd' (I. i. 188).
When Queen Margaret enters, a few lines later, she makes the cause of
this disaffection explicit.

Had I been there, which am a silly woman,
The soldiers should have toss'd me on their pikes
Before I would have granted to that act.
But thou preferr'st thy life before thine honour. . . .

(I. i. 243–6)

The audience that gathered to watch this effort of the fledgeling
Shakespeare to dramatize England's feudal wars thus saw, at the two
moments in the play which most control the course of the action, the

idea of honour dramatized as the principle of behaviour which most commands the characters' obedience, even when the issues of valid succession and of allegiance are at stake. The audience would not, in all likelihood, have thought this emphasis on honour unusual or contrived, for, by making honour the prevailing code of behaviour in the play, the young Shakespeare was putting on stage a set of ideas that were commonplace in the 1590s. Political, intellectual, and social life was so intertwined with and influenced by prevalent assumptions about honour that much artistic expression of that life inevitably deals with the intricate and contradictory roles honour was presumed to play in men's behaviour. Warwick, Henry's edgy allies, and all the other characters to whom Shakespeare assigns this commitment to honour must have seemed familiar, uncomplicated types to Shakespeare's earliest audience; they merely pronounce and demonstrate obedience to a code widely practised, often articulated, and seldom questioned. That audience would not, on the other hand, have found Henry quite so familiar a type, for Shakespeare has given the play its only substantial conflict other than those of a merely narrative kind by removing Henry from the otherwise prevalent context of honour. Hall's and Holinshed's Henry was overcome by Yorkist force and by Parliament; there is no hint that he is indifferent to, or incapable of, obeying the demands of honour. Shakespeare's Henry is troubled enough by his awareness that his claim rests on usurpation, and by Warwick's show of force, to ignore the honourable demand that he press his case; he is consequently so gentle that both his Queen and his momentary ally Warwick consider his presence on the battlefield an unwelcome cause of gentleness in their armies (II. i. 122–3 and II. v. 16–18); he, most significantly, counters Clifford's demand for honourable behaviour by asserting his preference for virtuous behaviour (II. ii. 43–53), a distinction which the sixteenth-century's most widely accepted definition of honour could not admit.

That audience, which saw this play early in the 1590s, and the audiences for which Shakespeare wrote his subsequent plays, nevertheless had, no doubt, mixed and changeable ideas about honour, for the idea was tirelessly debated and amplified in the few decades surrounding Shakespeare's plays.[2] The idea that honour is a reward granted to men who perform virtuous and generally beneficial deeds was, however, the most widely approved, and it was an idea formed by a characteristically eclectic blending of definitions provided by

Aristotle and Plato, illustrated by reference to historical example, and accommodated to orthodox Christianity. The most systematic presentation of this commonplace attitude towards honour is Robert Ashley's *Of Honour*, presented in manuscript form to Sir Thomas Egerton, Lord Keeper of the Great Seal, sometime between 1596 and 1603.[3] Ashley's dedicatory epistle to Egerton is a model of the orthodox assumptions about honour which the essay undertakes to support. Having justified his choice of the subject as 'some such piece of Philosophie ... most agreeable with the Rules of Religion, and most applyable to vse, and practise in our ciuile lyfe and conuersacion' and as the fittest subject, being 'the reward of virtue', he could offer his patron 'who by his vertuous deseruings (hauing tasted all the rewards of vertue ...) ys now become the most respected Censurer of all honorable, and dishonorable accions', Ashley explains that his motive for writing is to 'prove against the dull and heavye spirited, and against the abiect and base minded, that a moderate desire of Honor ys not only very conuenient, but also aboue all other good things (vertue only excepted which yt vsually accompanieth) to be preferred'.[4] Ashley is setting himself the task of defending the orthodox view against those of his contemporaries who either believe the pursuit of honour merely a mask for ambition – thus the qualifications of 'a moderate desire' – or believe honour to have no valid moral function – thus the insistence on the connection between honour and virtue. He might have chosen other adversaries, but, as we shall see, these two are the most prevalent sceptical judgments which sixteenth-century speculation about the idea reached. His purpose, therefore, and in general the purposes of most writers who discuss the idea of honour, is of a quite pragmatic and didactic kind. He is arguing the validity of the system of thought and behaviour which rewards – and has rewarded, in this instance, Sir Thomas Egerton – virtuous service with such tangible marks of honour as the Lord Keepership. The final chapter of the essay even touches on such day-by-day and relatively trivial ways of rendering honour as 'rising from [one's] seat ... attending, following, and accompanying ... [and] vncovering [one's head]'.[5] It is typical both of Ashley the humanist and of Ashley the apologist for honour that he should justify such a wide range of the theoretical and practical details of honour on 'grounds ... borrowed from the Peripatetick and Academick Philosophers'.[6]

That his grounds are considerably more Peripatetic than Academic is another mark of the faithfulness with which Ashley gives expression to the orthodox view. At the end of Chapter 2 of the essay, he does borrow a definition of the psychology of the honourable man from the ninth book of Plato's *Republic*,[7] but the definition of honour as the reward of virtue and the ethics of maintaining a moderate desire for honour, exposition of which provides most of the speculative part of the essay, are Aristotelian.

> *Honor* therefore ys a certeine testemonie of
> vertue shining of yt self, geven of some man
> by the iudgement of good men. . . .[8]

Something of the same sense of the term remains in present-day use, as when we mean by honour the respect due to worthy or honest actions, but what makes the idea loom so large in the minds of Ashley and his contemporaries is the integral role they see honour playing in the moral system of which it is a part. 'For how can vertue stand yf you take away honour?'[9] Ashley asks in his first, oratorical chapter. As the rest of his essay makes clear, he does not intend to suggest that honour should be sought for its own sake, but, rather, that honour, being an inevitable consequence of virtue, is an important motive for virtuous action.[10] 'But what better scope or end of this thing can there be then of vertue yt selfe . . . ?' Ashley asks in the chapter devoted to defining the term. 'Therfore we appoint the same end both of vertue and honour so that every vertue being referred to the cheefest good, honour also which ys the Companion of vertue shold be referred therevnto.'[11] Ashley has not defined the 'cheefest good', so the subtlety of the Aristotelian argument from which this is taken is lost,[12] not a surprising omission in an essay designed rather to justify a widely approved system of behaviour than to speculate on moral philosophy. His intent is to yoke virtue and honour, a yoking which in one form or another is the basis of the whole range of sixteenth- and seventeenth-century insistence on honourable behaviour. A man who performs a virtuous act is rewarded with honour, both in the intangible form of reputation and in the quite tangible form of preferment to a superior position, award of lands, or the like. This is precisely the form of honour, to take a Shakespearian instance, that Duncan knows he owes Macbeth for his martial success over the rebels. Macbeth has performed the virtuous act of protecting the state, and Duncan is made to give voice to the responsibility for honouring Macbeth which is now his. Ross, the messenger from Duncan, greets Macbeth as Thane of Cawdor, 'for an earnest of a greater honour' (I. iii. 104), and when Duncan appears Shakespeare emphasizes the responsibility to honour Macbeth which Duncan must now discharge.

> O worthiest cousin,
> The sin of my ingratitude even now
> Was heavy on me! Thou art so far before
> That swiftest wing of recompense is slow
> To overtake thee. Would thou hadst less deserv'd,
> That the proportion both of thanks and payment
> Might have been mine!
>
> (I IV. 14–20)

This, too, is the sort of honour represented by Sir Thomas's being made Lord Keeper. There have been no convenient wars, the most usual context for the virtuous pursuit of honour, so Egerton has been obliged, as Ashley remarks, to pass 'through all the most desired degrees of Honor which our peaceable gouerment doth afford, vnto a peaceable garment'.[13] All the public roles which a man might play are seen by various writers to afford opportunities for particular and specialized kinds of virtuous action, and consequently to provide for the award of specialized kinds of honour. Egerton's 'peaceable garment' is but one of these. Richard Hooker, in the process of justifying the award of marks of honour to ecclesiastics, categorizes a variety of such specialized roles by describing the various kinds of actions which, because beneficial, warrant honour.

> Which duty of every man towards all doth vary according to the several degrees whereby they are more or less beneficial, whom we do honour. 'Honour the physician,' saith the wise man: the reason why, because for necessities sake God created him. . . . Honour due to parents: the reason why because we have our beginning from them. . . . Honour due unto kings and governors: the reason why, because God hath set them 'for the punishment of evil doers, and for the praise of them that do well.' Thus we see by every of these particulars, that there is always some kind of virtue beneficial, wherein they excel who receive honour; and that degrees of honour are distinguished according to the value of those effects which the same beneficial virtue doth produce.[14]

It is consequently not surprising to find Ashley's final chapter dealing with apparently trivial means of rendering honour where it is due, for the orthodox attitude continually asserts that not only the speciality of rule, but also the speciality of every other role must be observed and that the reward of such observation is honour.

Castiglione, to cite one of the most elaborate descriptions of specialized virtues and rewards, has Lord Octavian, in the fourth book of *The Courtier*, explain at length what constitutes virtuous action in a courtier and how the honour received thereby differs from the honour due to a virtuous prince. The courtier's speciality is to 'enforme [the Prince] . . . of the truth of every matter meete for him to understand'. His responsibility is 'to disswade [the Prince] from every ill purpose, and to set him in the way of vertue', even – as with Kent's advising Lear to reconsider banishing Cordelia – when doing so runs counter to the Prince's resolve. 'And so shall the Courtier . . . understand how to behave himselfe . . . to drive into his Princes heade what honour and profit shall ensue to him and to his by justice, liberallitie, valiantness of courage, meekenesse, and by the other vertues that belong to a good prince. . . .' By doing this, Octavian asserts, the courtier 'deserve[s] much more praise and recompence, than for any other good worke that he can doe in the world'.[15] Castiglione has another, Lord Julian, object that Octavian's argument gives greater honour to the courtier than to the prince, for being the cause of the prince's virtues, he is 'also of a more worthiness than the Prince himselfe, which is most unfitting'.[16] Castiglione counters this argument by having Octavian appeal to the familiar idea of speciality. 'Vertue consisteth in doing and practise'. The courtier by his 'doing' inclines the prince to virtue and by and for that receives his honourable reward, but the prince can practise 'through his greatness' those virtues which the courtier has engendered in him.

Another of these specialized roles is that which women play. Most writers on the subject are agreed that a woman's chief obligation is to protect the honour implicit in her chastity, for she is incapable of positively gaining honour by performing virtuous deeds. Indeed, protecting that chastity is often thought possible only if the woman remain obedient to appropriate male authority, for unaided she is morally incapable of preserving her unique 'honour'. *The Courtiers Academie*, for instance, twice takes up the debate over the relative virtue and the consequent honour of which a woman is capable; each time the various courtiers pronounce the full range of traditional judgments, from those describing women as 'most imperfect creatures' and, slightly better, as 'an imperfect man', to this effort to praise her moral capacities.

> Though a woman have not mortall vertues in that perfection as hath a man, yet notwithstanding, that she also is indued with fortitude, justice, temperance, and with that prudence, which of it self is sufficient to obey well, towardes him that knoweth as well how to commande.[17]

The basic connection between virtuous action and the honour generated by it implicit in all these instances is Aristotelian in origin and present in most uses of the idea of honour, in whatever age. What gives such force to sixteenth-century uses of the idea is the pragmatic way in which its ethical implications are applied to the details of public and professional life. This combination produces a society in which each member can engage in the effort to perform his appropriate role in the expectation of appropriate honourable rewards both tangible and intangible, expectations justified – no matter how grandiose or trivial – by being an integral part of that society's most pervasive ethical system. All actions, consequently, take on moral implications of a more public and universal sort than they would otherwise have, a condition which may help to explain the ease with which much Renaissance literature, particularly the drama, makes ethical allegory out of the most realistic of actions. Certainly Henry VI's refusal to risk his life for honour's sake is not dramatized as an act of individual cowardice; Shakespeare, rather, exploits the dilemma implicit in orthodox assumptions about the ethics of honour. Henry knows his claim is shaky; he prefers virtuous to honourable action; and some of the central conflicts of the play depend on Shakespeare's having given him the uncanny and quite unusual capacity to see that virtuous and honourable behaviour are not necessarily the same. It is a revolutionary insight.

Side by side with this widely held assumption that honour is the reward due to virtue there is in most writers about the idea and in most practitioners of its tenets a clear awareness of the single abuse to which the desire for honour is most subject. The ambitious man might desire more honour than he deserves, or desire it for the wrong reasons. Aristotle's ethics of mediocrity is the origin of all sixteenth-century justifications of a moderate desire for honour, and Ashley's essay typically claims classical authority for this justification. 'Although I cold bring plentifull proofes out of Peripatetike Philosophers,' Ashley remarks, 'That there ys a certeine vertue conuersant in moderating the desire of honour ... yet reason yt self doth teach yt. ...'[18] The danger particularly inherent in ambition is that the man greedy for honour will pursue it for itself rather than pursuing virtue. Ashley lists several historical examples of this vice, among them the story of Caesar's weeping upon comparing his exploits with Alexander's. 'Was not [Caesar] arrogant and insolent herein,' Ashley asks, 'which wold not so much imitate his vertue, yf any were, as envy his great fame and renowne?' That 'yf any were' is a serious disclaimer, for Ashley's next example is Alexander's bewailing his failure to become lord of even one of the many worlds Democritus posited. 'What yf [Alexander] had gotten ... all the whole world and those infinite other worlds which *Democritus* imagined, had he bene any ... worthyer of honour, which ys not seen in this swelling of the mind, but in the brightness of vertue?' Ashley's Aristotelian heritage shows on every page. Virtue consists in action; the reward of that action is honour; to pursue more honour than virtuous action warrants or to pursue honour for its own sake is a vice. 'Therefore such ought never to be the true desire of honour as these men [Caesar, Alexander, etc.] had, least we fall into the vice of ambition whiles we thincke to mainteyne a certeine greatnes and worthynes of mind.'[19] A letter from Queen Elizabeth to Lord Mountjoy, then her Lord Deputy in Ireland, reveals how readily and completely the intricate theories of honour and the danger of its attendant vice, ambition, became the norm of public behaviour. In a note in her own hand, a device the Queen used with particular effectiveness again and again to encourage support from the recipient of such a mark of honour, Elizabeth assures Mountjoy that although he thinks he is being adversely criticized at home, 'there is no louder trump that may sound out your praise, your hazard, your care, your luck, than we have blasted in all our Court and elsewhere in deed'. She can only attribute his suspicion that he is being dispraised to a 'melancholy humour', which she in turn attributes to 'God's good Providence for you, that (lest all these glories might elevate you too much) He hath suffered (though not made) such a scruple to keep you under His rod, Who best knows we have more need of bits than spurs'.[20]

The contrary vice, to desire less honour than one deserves, is an inevitable part of the ethics of mediocrity, but it nowhere gets the same attention as ambition. Ashley gives the problem one sentence in his chapter on the moderate desire for honour, and, interestingly enough, used that sentence to attack the Stoics as being guilty of a defective desire for honour, 'Neither ys the *Cynike Diogenes* or any other *Stoyck* which contemneth honour to be commended as modest in avoyding of ambition, since that true moderation consistes not either in suppressing and hiding of vertue or in not knowing the force and valew thereof. . . .'[21] Ambition, not undue humility, or '*Pusillanimitie*', as Ashley has it, is the most enticing vice to which the honourable man is subject, and apologists for the ethic of honour rarely concern themselves with its defect. Imaginative literature, too, rarely exploits the ethical dilemma inherent in a defective desire for honour, a fact which must reflect the prevalent tendency to see ambition as the potential flaw in the system. Henry VI's allies, to be sure, consider him to be defective in his desire for honour, and Falstaff will later reject the demands of the code out of hand, but Shakespeare gives both characters a considerably more intricate response to the demands of honour than mere cowardice, or *Pusillanimitie*, could provide.

This delicately balanced system survived some extraordinarily hard use, for even the most resourceful and strong-willed inhabitants of Elizabeth's England had somehow to accommodate their actions to a system which expected beneficial service to the common good to be every man's motive, however much honourable reward he thereby expected. *The Courtiers Academie*, translated into English in 1598, expresses the sort of commitment to the general good which was commonly expected of those who pursued honour. That man, one of the courtiers asserts, who through 'viliere hazardeth not his life, for Religion, his Countrie, Prince, and Friends, commiteth an unjust fact: for a man not being borne to himself, but for all these, defraudeth [all these] of that which is their proper good: and therefore as unjust hee is worthy of infamie. . . .'[22] That even the most significant events of Elizabeth's reign are so peculiarly the result of individual effort on the part of her commanders, courtiers, and other subjects may in part be accounted for by this pervasive system that demanded service to the country in the expectation of honourable reward. Many of Elizabeth's letters show how thoroughly she understood the system, and how clearly she recognized both her responsibilities under the system and the opportunity it provided her to control her subjects' behaviour.

Elizabeth, for instance, responded to the success of her commander in the field, Henry Carey, Lord Hunsdon, over Leonard Dacres' rebel forces, in what was to be the only actual battle of the Northern Rebellion of 1569–70, by having Burghley draft a letter of praise to Hunsdon. It seems fulsome enough.

> We will not now by words express how inwardly glad we are that you have had such success, whereby your courage in such an unequal match, your faithfulness and your wisdom is seen to the world, this being the first fight in field in our time against rebels; but we mean also by just reward to let the world see how much we esteem such a service as this is, and we would have you thank God heartily, and comfort yourself with the assurance of our favour.[23]

But the Queen awarded Hunsdon a mark of particular distinction by adding one of the postscripts she used so effectively, touching on the honour he had gained for himself by serving her so well.

> I doubt much, my Harry, whether that the victory were given me more joyed me, or that you were by God appointed the instrument of my glory; and I assure you for my country's good, the first might suffice, but for my heart's contentation, the second more pleased me. It likes me not a little that, with a good testimony of your faith, there is seen a stout courage of your mind, that more trusted to the goodness of your quarrel than to the weakness of your number. Well, I can say no more, *beatus est ille seruus quem, cum Dominus uenerit, inuenerit faciendo sua mandata*; and that you may not think that you have done nothing for your profit, though you have done much for honour, I intend to make this journey somewhat to increase your livelihood, that you may not say to yourself, *perditur quod factum est ingrato.*
>
> Your loving kinswoman,
Elizabeth R.[24]

In 1575 she assured Walter Devereux, 1st Earl of Essex, that although he had been again removed from command of the Irish expedition, the service he had done her in his quest for honour would be appropriately rewarded.

> If lines could value life, or thanks could answer praise, I should esteem my pen's labour the best employed time that many years hath

lent me. But to supply the want that both these carrieth, a right judgement of upright dealing shall lengthen the scarcity that either of the other wanted. Deem, therefore, Cousin mine, that the search of your honour, with the danger of your breath, hath not been bestowed on so ungrateful a Prince that will not both consider the one and reward the other.

Your most loving cousin and Sovereign,
E.R.[25]

Royal letters of this sort, both playful and portentous in tone, are common, and they reveal how habitually the Queen understood her subjects' actions in terms of the honour they expected for the service they had rendered. This system of honour was clearly a most widely accepted norm, the precepts of which had a pervasive and detailed effect on the way people behaved. Recalling a few details from the careers of two of the most illustrious and independent of Elizabeth's subjects can provide a fairly clear sense of the grip this system had on men's minds in the sixteenth century. More disparate personalities than those of Philip Sidney and the 2nd Earl of Essex would be difficult to imagine; yet they shared a deep-seated commitment to the same principles of honour, and the effect of this commitment is displayed in detail in their actions. Sidney, the idol of his age, is not a surprising instance of honourable behaviour. It is, indeed, as the 'mirror of honour' that such 'remembrances' as George Whetstone's praise his exemplary behaviour. But a clearer view of the hold which the principles of honour had on that behaviour may be gained by recalling some details of Greville's biography. Greville writes the biography, as he remarks, 'to the end that in the tribute I owe him, our nation may see a sea-mark, rais'd upon their native coast . . . and so by a right meridian line of their own, learn to sayl through the straits of True Vertue, into a calm and spacious ocean of humane honour'.[26] Chapters 2 and 3 maintain at length that honour in an extraordinary degree was due to Sidney because he was extraordinarily beneficial to the state, the church, his friends, etc. One typical judgment: 'it will be confessed by all men, that this one man's example and personall respect, did not onely encourage Learning and Honour in the schooles, but brought the affection and true use thereof both into the court and camp'.[27] Most of the details of Greville's account are familiar, and such incidents as Sidney's treatment of the insult he received from the Earl of Oxford and, indeed, Greville's version of the manner of Sidney's death display the workings of the ideal of honour in this celebrated, but not atypical, member of Elizabeth's court. Perhaps the most revealing incident of all, however, is found in Greville's account of a private conversation with Sidney. Greville reports being entrusted by the Prince of Orange to convey messages to Elizabeth regarding various weighty matters touching the imperialistic ambitions of the 'Popish and Spanish' courts. William took the occasion to deliver 'his free expressing of himselfe in the honor of Sir Philip Sidney. . . .'[28] The Prince understood Sidney to be unemployed under Elizabeth, and charged Greville to deliver to the Queen his judgment that 'her Majesty had one of the ripest and greatest councellors of estate in Sir Philip Sidney that at this day lived in Europe', to which judgment 'hee was pleased to leave his owne credit engaged, untill her Majesty might please to employ this gentleman, either amongst her friends or enemies'. Greville, 'thinking to make the finespun threads of friendship more firm between them [i.e. William and Sidney]', reported William's judgment to Sidney before doing so to Elizabeth, but Sidney forbade his making the report to the Queen for two reasons which are honourable in the most orthodox and optimistic sense of the term. Honour is the reward of virtue, which consists in action; Sidney therefore forbade Greville's report, 'for the Queen had the life it self [i.e. Sidney] daily attending her: and if she either did not or could not value it so high, the commendation of that worthy prince could be no more . . . than a lively picture of that life, and so of far lesse credit and estimation with her'. Second, his understanding of the system of virtuous service and honourable reward according to which the realm operates, and of his responsibility to protect the Queen's role in this system, recognized that Orange's message is something of an affront to Elizabeth, for 'princes love not that forrain Powers should have extraordinary interest in their subjects; much lesse to be taught by them how they should place their own: as arguments either upbraiding ignorance, or lack of large rewarding goodness in them'.[29] The 'large rewarding goodness' of the parsimonious Elizabeth, which was no doubt a carefully manipulated part of her political acumen, and Sidney's insistence that honour must be justified by deeds are the mainstays of the system; that Sidney should obey its tenets even in the privacy of a conversation with his friend – or, even granting Greville license to varnish his friend's image, that Greville should do so by making him perfectly honourable in the

23

most orthodox sense of the term – speaks of the immediate relevance of the system to the day-by-day thoughts and actions of sixteenth-century Englishmen.

More complicated but as telling is Elizabeth's constant effort to control Essex's increasingly aberrant career by carefully awarding his accomplishments, then denying his failures, appropriate marks of honour. Much of the orderliness of Elizabeth's court depended on her capacity to award or withhold honour, and her presumably romantic affection for Essex never diminished this capacity. The height of Essex's military successes was certainly the Cadiz expedition of 1596, one of the rewards of which was his being appointed commander of the so-called Island Voyage in 1597. This expedition against the Azores was unsuccessful, and various accounts of the voyage emphasize the quarrel between Essex and Raleigh which marked it, a quarrel consistently argued in terms of the relative honour due to both. 'Raleigh', as Camden reports one incident, 'out of necessity of taking in fresh water, the opportunity of the time, and desire of a little glory . . .' seized an enemy fortification in Essex's absence. 'Sir Gilly Merris', on Essex's arrival, 'informed him what *Raleigh* had done; and persuaded him that Raleigh had seyzed upon the towne to no other end, but to prevent Essex, of the glory. . . .' Essex was easy to persuade, Camden asserts in a statement neatly reminiscent of the Aristotelian definition of honour, for he was 'greedy of glory, out of a desire bred in magnanimous spirits, and knew well Raleigh's ambitious mind. . . .'[30] Other affronts awaited Essex on his return to England. Elizabeth had made Charles Howard, who had commanded the English fleet against the Armada, Earl of Nottingham, but the charter granting him the Earldom contained a clause which Essex saw as yet another diminution of his own honour. Howard, as the charter read, '*ioyntly with our most deare Cousin* Robert *Earle of* Essex, *had valiently and honourably taken* . . . *the Isle and City of* Gadiz. . . ., Essex, 'who challenged that glory wholly to himself', took the charter 'as done in disgrace of him'. He also 'interpreted it to be to his prejudice, that the Admirall, who whilest he was a Baron was inferiour to him in honour, now being created an Earle, he went before him in the prerogative of honour. . . .'[31] The Queen in 1597 was still supporting her brilliant young favourite, and Camden's record makes it clear that she knew that it was Essex's honour which that support must prop up.

But the Queene, who alwaies was both a Favourer and an amplifier of *Essex* his honour, to pacifie his displeasure, and withall provide for his honour ... honoured him with the title of Earle Marshall of England. ...[32]

But darker days for Essex were, of course, ahead. After the celebrated incident in which Essex angered the Queen, received a cuff on the ear from her for his pains, and dared to put his hand to his sword, the Queen punished him not with imprisonment but with the dishonour implicit in denying him access to the court. Reconciled and sent to Ireland as commander of the English forces, Essex disobeyed the Queen's instructions, wasted his men and supplies, failed miserably with the expedition, and returned unbidden to England. Punishment for this included a brief period of imprisonment, but the most galling response of the Queen's was apparently her refusal to allow him to return to court even after his release from confinement. As the Queen began to withdraw her 'large rewarding goodness' from his mounting disobedience, Essex stumbled into the course of active opposition which cost him his head. The desire for honour is of course not the only motive nor the manipulation of honourable reward the only issue in this most complicated and affecting event of Elizabeth's final years, but throughout Essex's fall, as during his ascendancy, traditional assumptions about honour are so intermingled with the motives and actions of all the participants that the hold which these assumptions had on men's minds is indisputable. This habit of mind is a much more relevant and immediate source for such plays as Shakespeare's second chronicle cycle than any presumed similarity between Bolingbroke's usurpation and Essex's rebellion, for, clearly, one of the formative principles of Shakespeare's treatment of those feudal wars is his concern to treat them in terms of Tudor political ideals, significant among which is the ideal of honour.

As this blend of Aristotelian and Platonic definitions was the idea of honour most commonly examined in theory and most affective of behaviour, it is naturally the form of the idea most often examined by Renaissance artists. There were, however, other formulations of the idea of honour, most of which remained peripheral to English life and, thus, to letters, however profound the effect of these formulations became as the humanist tradition dissipated. Calvin turns his attention to the problem of honour from time to time in the *Institutes*, and characteristically asserts that since man is incapable of virtuous action without the operation of God's special grace, to honour the man for that action were impiety.

> [Man] cannot claim for himself ever so little beyond what is rightfully his without losing himself in vain confidence and without usurping God's honour, and thus becoming guilty of monstrous sacrilege.[33]

In another place, examining whether moral integrity and the pursuit of virtue in Camillus, a pagan, do not argue that human nature has the ability to cultivate virtue, Calvin again ascribes whatever virtues Camillus displays to 'special graces of God, which he bestows . . . upon men otherwise wicked'. Honour therefore plays a deleterious role, for it wrongly implies that man is himself capable of virtuous action, for which he can expect reward, an expectation which foments ambition.

> But because, however excellent anyone has been, his own ambition always pushes him on – a blemish with which all virtues are so sullied that before God they lose all favour – anything in profane men that appears praiseworthy must be considered worthless.[34]

The Stoic rejection of honour was based on quite different grounds, grounds which, of course, show none of the '*Pusillanimitie*' of which Ashley had accused the Stoics. To the degree that an honourable reputation depends on someone else's recognition of one's virtues, the Stoic considers that reputation morally irrelevant. Guillaume DuVair's *Moral Philosophie of the Stoicks* was translated into English in 1598 and again in 1664, so serves as a convenient instance of what Englishmen considered neo-Stoical thought to be. When describing honour as a reward external to the man honoured, DuVair asserts that 'riches, reputation, and briefly, that which doth no way depend of our willes'[35] are matters which we should consequently neither seek nor despair at not obtaining. These and other, less coherently organized rejections of the orthodox ethic of honour[36] rarely found their way into imaginative literature, but side by side with the orthodox formulation of the ethic of honour there did exist a quite different and compelling set of assumptions about honour, assumptions which did become important themes in the work of Shakespeare and many of his contemporaries.

The orthodox idea, however elaborately it was expressed or observed, remained Aristotelian in its assumption that honour is something external to man which may be gained only by virtuously performing appropriate deeds; this other, most significant of the unorthodox attitudes towards honour regarded it rather as an innate moral capacity than as external reward for virtuous action. The difference is an important one, for rather than encouraging action judged virtuous by a widely understood and carefully defined ethical system, this other attitude towards honour provides a basis for an entirely subjective and personal ethic. Chapman is the playwright contemporary with Shakespeare who concerns himself most consistently with the implications of this idea, but Shakespeare, too, beginning with *Julius Caesar*, puts this decadent form of the idea of honour to elaborate dramatic use.

One applies the term *decadent* to this form of honour only hesitantly, but since it cannot be identified with any particular philosophic tradition, a precisely descriptive term cannot be found. Whenever the idea appears, however, it is coupled with the assumption that the world is in moral decay, a condition which only this private sense of what is right – i.e. honour – can alleviate. Thus those men who possess this sense of honour must obey its dictates at all costs, even if the action thus generated be contrary to more public and widespread principles of behaviour. The origins of this idea are obscure, but occasionally such books as *The Courtiers Academie* give voice to an attitude which may be seen as the transition which was necessary for this different idea of honour to develop from the older, Aristotelian formulation. Late in the book devoted to a definition of honour, Romei has his courtiers argue whether the code requires the honourable man to maintain a quarrel in which he knows himself to be in the wrong. Romei's argument has consistently been orthodox, but here he has Gualinguo, the chief spokesman in the definition of honour, assert that all those 'which heretofore have written of honor ... are fallen into manifest errors', for otherwise 'they would not have saide, that an honorable man ought not to maintain an unjust quarrell, for preservation of his honor. ...' Men desiring to be honoured, Gualinguo continues, 'must indevour by right and wrong, not to lose that opinion and supposition wherewith they are borne. ...'[37] This argument provides, at least, a way in which honour can be seen as a system of value independent of orthodox ethics and so marks a break from the Aristotelian tradition, which insistently yokes honour with virtue. Similarly, though he reaches entirely different conclusions, DuVair distinguishes between that honour worthless to the Stoic because it comes from without and that which he sees as an individual sense of what is right. The Aristotelian idea dies hard, and there are echoes of it in DuVair, but his intent is clearly to accommodate to Stoical principles the idea that honour is some sort of individual moral perception in a world in general decay. Honour 'dooth wholly depend on vs', DuVair remarks. 'If wee once forsake it, wee doe but ... fasten the rest of our minds vpon the opinion of the vulgar sort of people, and so ... renounce our liberties, to serue the humours and passions of other men ... and wee loue not vertue, but as the common people doe loue and fauour it. ...'[38] Later in the same argument, DuVair reflects the Aristotelian definition by asserting that 'there is no true honor in the world but that which commeth from vertue,' but then displays his different understanding of honour – and his Stoical intentions – by remarking that 'vertue seeks no greater or ampler theater to shew her selfe in, then her owne conscience. The higher the Sunne is the lesse shadow it makes, and the greater a mans vertue is the lesse glorie it seekes.'[39]

One finds speculation about the aberrant idea of honour largely in such instances as these, where the idea is being accommodated to other purposes; there is no explicit, independent definition of the idea. Ruth Kelso, in her excellent study of the standards of gentlemanly conduct in the 1600s, argues that the idea developed as a justification, among gentlemen, of the officially illegal duel. Quoting Fausto de Longiano, she neatly recalls the most widespread philosophical justification of this extension of the meaning of honour.

The law of honor ... 'is founded on the most solid foundation, which is reason and which cannot be destroyed. It is immutable and external, not subject to the changes of time, and therefore it cannot receive diverse interpretations. It has been approved by the universal consent of all men, and of all ages. It began with the beginning of the world, and will endure while the world endures. Everyone is held to the observance of this law, but the civil law is not observed except in the most limited part of the inhabited earth'. The law of honor was thus practically identified with the law of nature ... which, as it was usually defined, was the moral law, made known by reason, inviting man to do good through certain practical principles implanted in all men, such as to reverence God ... etc. The law of nature was in other words the absolute standard of goodness.[40]

The same assumption that Miss Kelso cites in Fausto de Longiano is present in Rabelais' definition of the honour peculiar to the Thelemites.

> Because men *that are free, well-born, well-bred,* and conversant in honest companies, have naturally an *instinct* and spur that prompteth them into virtuous actions, and withdraws them from vice, which is called *honour.*[41]

Burckhardt, one of the first modern scholars to note the implications of this extension of the meaning of honour, sees this as 'that enigmatic mixture of conscience and egoism which often survives in the modern man after he has lost . . . faith, love, and hope',[42] and it is apparent that those who turned to an individual sense of honour as the chief moral guide did so in despair over the moral disarray of their world.

Little direct evidence is available of the effect this aberrant idea of honour had on the public and private lives of Renaissance Englishmen. Since each effort to explain the sudden increase in duelling on James I's accession is as partial as the next, one may as well surmise, with Miss Kelso, that it was connected with this aberrant idea of honour. The effective system of honourable reward for service done the state in Elizabeth's time to a large degree depended on the identification of Elizabeth *as* the state, an identification which consistently escaped the Stuarts' most strenuous efforts. In the absence of such a norm – of such 'large rewarding goodness', as Sidney put it – the impulse to prove that one was one of those honourable men who possessed such special capacities must have been compelling. There is a gulf between the Aristotelian definition of honour as the reward due to virtue and Romei's argument that the honourable man must endeavour 'by right and wrong' to defend his honour; one can easily step from Romei's argument to the idea that the honourable man has an innate capacity to see what is right and a moral responsibility to enact that right, even if the act be counter to more public and widespread definitions of right and wrong.

Only one contemporary treatise explicitly surveys the various and contradictory ideas about honour which sixteenth- and seventeenth-century Englishmen inherited or developed for themselves. The main intent of Greville's *Inquisition upon Fame and Honour* is to reject the various claims for honour on a Calvin-like basis that only God deserves honour. He describes the Aristotelian idea exactly, for he sees as its basis the conjunction which 'the father of Philosophie' made between the virtue of 'magnanimity' and its honourable reward.[43] But he denies, like Calvin, that the virtue resides in the man.

> Let truth examine where this vertue liues,
> And hold it vaine, if not produc'd in act;
> Man is corrupt, and no perfection giues,
> What euer in him others praise enact:
>   So as if *Fame* be vnto goodnesse due;
>   It onely can in God, be great and true. . . .
>
> (Stanza 32)

He further 'vrge[s] against this masters grounds,/That our first Adam, imag'd is to vs' in those, among them the Bishop of Rome, who usurp God's place by claiming honour. Nor will the Stoic formulation of honour serve. Greville does not, with Ashley, see it as *'Pusillanimitie'*; he sees it as hypocrisy.

> For *Fame* they still oppose euen from those grounds,
> That proue as truely all things else as vaine.
> They giue their vertues onely humane bounds,
> And without God subuert to build againe
>   Refin'd *Ideas*, more than flesh can beare,
>   All foule within, yet speake as God were there.
>
> (Stanza 22)

He even considers the aberrant idea of creating honour as a standard of behaviour in a decadent world, and though Greville's may be a Calvinist's despair, he does view this god which man has created for himself as having some practical use in a world from which the true God is absent. Though men's lives are 'but *labyrinths of error,/Shops of deceit, and Seas of Misery*', Greville's first stanza asserts, and since death 'yeelds so small comfort', men are attracted to life by the illusions: '*Gaine, Honour, Pleasure*'.

> Of which three baytes, yet *Honour* seemes the chiefe,
> And is vnto the world, like goodly weather,
> Which giues the spirits life, the thoughts reliefe,
> Delight, and trauell reconciles together:
>   So as the Learn'd, and Great, no more admire it,
>   Then euen the silly Artisans aspire it.
>
> (Stanza 2)

Man, Greville argues, has thus created an entirely subjective system of value, in the absence of an objective one, and acts as though it were valid. This is not the best response to the world's decadence, Greville later in the treatise argues; faith is. But it is a response in which Greville, parting company with Calvin, sees a kind of practical value.

> For to be good the world finds it too hard,
> And to be nothing to subsistence is
> A fatall, and unnaturing award;
> So as betweene perfection, and vnblisse,
>   Man, out of man, will make himselfe a frame,
>   Seekes outward helpe, and borrowes that of *Fame*.

(Stanza 19)

When one realizes that the man who here sees honour as only a sort of stopgap effort to accommodate man's depravity nevertheless chose the orthodox, Aristotelian ideal of honour as the most appropriate standard for measuring his friend Sidney's exemplary life, one becomes aware of how habitually Shakespeare's contemporaries turned to these complexly mingled ideas about honour when they were concerned to describe or understand human behaviour. Shakespeare's emphasis on honour as a motive for behaviour in such early plays as *3 Henry IV* reflects this habit of mind, and it is only a beginning.

Notes to Chapter 1

[1] All quotations of Shakespeare are from *The Complete Works of Shakespeare*, eds. Irving Ribner and George Lyman Kittredge (Waltham, Mass., 1971).

[2] There is one book-length treatment of these ideas and of Shakespeare's use of them, Curtis Brown Watson's *Shakespeare and the Renaissance Concept of Honor* (Princeton, 1960). As Paul N. Siegel has pointed out, however, in 'Shakespeare and the Neo-Chivalric Cult of Honor', *The Centennial Review of Arts and Science*, VIII (1964), 39–70, Watson's book introduces as much confusion as it does clarity into the study of Renaissance ideas of honour. Watson's survey of Classical, Medieval, and Renaissance formulations of the idea is thorough, and provides convenient access to widely scattered material,

but his thesis, that most aspects of honour belong uniquely to the ethics of 'pagan humanism' and so are incompatible with the ethics of Christianity, and his practice, using sections of the plays to illustrate the various categories of honour he has described, do confuse the matter. In his effort to dichotomize, Watson fails to consider Christian uses of classical formulations of the idea which such theologians as Richard Hooker make, and he disregards those portions of secular arguments which claim a Christian origin for human honour. Robert Ashley, for instance, easily accommodates the Aristotelian definition to a Christian context by writing, 'so must I fetch the beginning of Honour from God' (*Of Honour*, ed. Virgil B. Heltzel [San Marino, 1947], p. 27). In Part II, Watson draws passages from the plays to support such arguments as this: 'The Renaissance concept of Nobility, defined at the beginning of Chapter 4, is most clearly exemplified in Shakespeare's plays by his characterization of Brutus, "the noblest Roman of them all"'. Watson's technique consistently is to cite passages from the plays as evidence that Shakespeare reflects the various categories of honour defined by Part I of the book. Siegel's critical technique, which is to examine Shakespeare's use of honour in *1 Henry IV*, *Troilus and Cressida*, *All's Well That Ends Well*, *Coriolanus*, and *Timon of Athens*, focuses more rewardingly on the place honour occupies in the whole dramatic pattern of those plays, but – even with Watson's example before him – Siegel gives way to the temptation to dichotomize. Siegel, too, finds 'two opposing Renaissance concepts of honor' (p. 40), and though his description of various attitudes towards honour is more exact than Watson's, his distinction between the 'Christian humanist ideal of honor' and the 'neo-chivalric cult of honor' is rather imposed than innate. Everyone who reads the courtesy books, duelling treatises, 'Remembrances' of notable men, and various educational treatises, such as the *Book of the Courtier* or *The Courtiers Academie*, which form the basic library of Renaissance books about honour, is no doubt tempted to place the various attitudes he discovers into one categorical system or another. But the origins of the idea are eclectic and its effects many and varied; to impose categories on such a set of ideas is inevitably to oversimplify. Siegel's distinction, for instance, between 'the Italianates at the Elizabethan court headed by the Earl of Oxford' as 'the most dedicated devotees of the neo-chivalric cult of honor' (p. 41), and the 'new ideal of the courtier, in which the virtues of the humanistic scholar ... are united with those of the medieval knight' as the 'ideal which governed the new Tudor aristocracy' (pp. 40–1), ignores the evidence that the basic effort of the neo-chivalric code, especially under Elizabeth, was to glorify the monarch. The various members of Elizabeth's court, from the 'humanist' Sidney to the 'Italianate' Oxford, as Siegel would have it, participated actively in the Queen's Accession Day tilts, certainly a more identifiable part of neo-chivalry than a personal sensitivity to one's honour. Siegel admits that 'the writers of the dueling treatises [which in his view expound the neo-chivalric cult] made frequent reference to a few quotations from Aristotle and the writers of the courtesy books [which in his view expound the Christian humanist ideal] incorporated elements of the chivalric ideal', but, he concludes, 'the primacy of the chivalric tradition for the neo-chivalric cult of honor and of classical philosophy for the Christian humanist ideal of honor is clear enough' (p. 41). Renaissance speculation about honour, however, is not confined to such dichotomized categories, and it is unlikely that the men of the sixteenth and seventeenth centuries thought of honour in such terms. It is even more unlikely that such categories would have enjoyed wide enough currency to permit Shakespeare's use of them in a series of plays, widely separated in time. C. L. Barber's thorough statistical study of the changing meanings of the word, *Honour in English Drama, 1591–1700* (Göteborg, 1957), is unfortunately of limited value to students of the plays because his methods require him to 'disregard the attitude of the dramatist himself to honour, his implicit and explicit comments on the ideal' (p. 37).

Watson lists fifty-eight 'Works by Renaissance Authors' in a bibliography appended to *Shakespeare and the Renaissance Concept of Honor*, though some of the works are concerned only tangentially with honour. Reviewing Watson in *Shakespeare Quarterly*, XIII (1962), 357, Sears Jayne notes two English and six continental discussions of the idea which Watson overlooked. Sir James Turner, *Pallas Armata* (1683), Geffrey Whitney, *A Choice of Emblemes* (1586), and George Whetstone, *A Remembrance of the Life, Death, and Vertues of the Most Noble and Honourable Lord Thomas late Erle of Sussex . . .* (1583), which titles neither Watson nor Jayne mention, are also explicitly concerned with the idea of honour, and add weight to the sheer numerical evidence of Renaissance interest in the subject.

[3] Robert Ashley, *Of Honour*, ed. Virgil Heltzel (San Marino, 1947). Heltzel believes the essay to have been prepared for Egerton's predecessor and presented to Egerton soon after his appointment to the office in May of 1596. See the Introduction, p. 18.

[4] Ashley, p. 24.

[5] Ashley, p. 71.

[6] Ashley, p. 24.

[7] Ashley, p. 40 and n. 28.

[8] Ashley, p. 34. Heltzel cites (n. 17) the *Rhetoric*, I, v, 8–9 here, but the assumption is basic to all of Aristotle's statements on honour in both the *Rhetoric* and the *Nicomachean Ethics*.

[9] Ashley, p. 28.

[10] Watson (p. 6) cites this query as evidence that the 'Renaissance code of honor teaches . . . that it is one of man's primary obligations to act so that he wins the esteem and the praise of his fellow men.'

[11] Ashley, pp. 37–8.

[12] The argument is developed in Book I of the *Nicomachean Ethics*.

[13] Ashley, p. 24.

[14] Richard Hooker, *Of the Laws of Ecclesiastical Polity*, Bk. VII, Ch. xvii, Sec. 4; in *The Works of . . . Richard Hooker*, ed. John Keble (New York, 1845; Ilkley, 1969).

[15] Baldassare Castiglione, *The Book of the Courtier*, tr. Sir Thomas Hoby, 1561, ed. Ernest Rhys (London: Everyman's Library, 1928), p. 265.

[16] Castiglione, p. 296.

[17] Count Annibale Romei, *The Courtiers Academie*, tr. John Kepers (the copy in the British Museum is not dated, but Valentine Sims had a license to print this title in 1598), p. 235. Watson, citing *The Courtiers Academie*'s definition of 'honor feminine' as a quality which 'is preserved by not failing onely in one of their proper particular vertues, which is honestie', provides a brief but detailed summary of sixteenth-century statements on the subject (pp. 159–62). When he turns to Shakespeare's use of these ideas (pp. 437–47), however, Watson argues that 'as in so many other instances, Shakespeare makes use of this moral commonplace in his drama almost without alteration' (pp. 437–8). This argument, as I hope to demonstrate, does a disservice to the quality of Shakespeare's thought.

[18] Ashley, p. 41.

[19] Ashley, pp. 45–6.

[20] G. B. Harrison, ed., *The Letters of Queen Elizabeth I* (New York, 1968; London, 1968), p. 289. Hereafter cited as Elizabeth.

[21] Ashley, p. 46.

[22] Romei, p. 105.

[23] Elizabeth, pp. 82–3.

[24] Elizabeth, p. 83.

[25] Elizabeth, p. 125.

[26] Fulke Greville, *The Life of the Renowned Sr. Philip Sidney*, in *The Works . . . of Fulke Greville*, ed. Alexander Grosart (New York, 1966), IV.7. Hereafter cited as *Life of Sidney*.

[27] *Life of Sidney*, p. 38.

[28] *Life of Sidney*, p. 29.

[29] *Life of Sidney*, p. 31.

[30] William Camden, *Annals*, tr. R. N. (London, 1635), p. 473.

[31] Camden, p. 476.

[32] Camden, p. 476.

[33] John Calvin, *Institutes of the Christian Religion*, tr. Ford L. Battles, ed. John T. McNeill (Philadelphia, 1960), II.ii.10; tr. Beveridge (Cambridge, 1957).

[34] Calvin, II.iii.4. See also II.ii.17, nn. 63 and 64.

[35] Guillaume DuVair, *The Moral Philosophie of the Stoicks*, tr. Thomas James (1598), ed. Rudolf Kirk (New Brunswick, 1951), p. 68.

[36] Hiram Haydn, *The Counter-Renaissance* (New York, 1960), pp. 555–618, summarizes the 'disillusioned' responses to the idea of honour.

[37] Romei, p. 100.

[38] DuVair, pp. 78–9.

[39] DuVair, p. 80.

[40] Ruth Kelso, *The Doctrine of the English Gentleman in the Sixteenth Century*, University of Illinois Studies in Language and Literature, XIV (Urbana, 1929), p. 42.

[41] Haydn (p. 573) cites this passage as evidence of an aristocratic and courtly 'tendency to think of "honor" as an innate quality' rather than as a reward due to virtue.

[42] Jacob Burckhardt, *The Civilization of the Renaissance in Italy*, tr. S. G. C. Middlemore (London, 1928), p. 433.

[43] Fulke Greville, *An Inquisition upon Fame and Honour*, Stanza 31. All quotations of the poem are from *Poems and Dramas of Fulke Greville*, ed. Geoffrey Bullough (New York, 1945), Vol. I.

Chapter 2

I HENRY IV
The Mirror up to Honour

The first time that Shakespeare gives a play its basic form and defines the action of the principal characters by reference to the idea of honour is in *1 Henry IV*. Important moments in the action of the *Henry VI* plays are expressed in terms of honour, and such familiar moments in *Richard II* as Mowbray's appeal to honour to justify his refusal to allow King Richard to reconcile his quarrel with Bolingbroke and York's demand that King Henry put Aumerle, York's son, to death for treason to protect the family honour demonstrate how effectively Shakespeare could turn the dilemma implicit in the codes of honour to dramatic account. But in *1 Henry IV*, for the first time, the structure of the play depends not so much on a narrative development of military reversals, as in *3 Henry VI*, nor so much on the unfortunate fall of one character and attendant rise of another, as in *Richard II*, as it does on the quite distinct responses Shakespeare has the principal characters make to honour, the nominal ethic of the play.

Indeed, the idea that Shakespeare arranges the three principals of *1 Henry IV* in a quasi-Aristotelian paradigm of the theme of honour has been so often iterated and has so dominated the teaching of the play that it has become a virtual truism. Hotspur, the argument goes, represents the excess, Falstaff the defect, and Hal the virtuous mean of the honorable man.[1] This reading of the play, however, obscures Shakespeare's intent, for, although it is clear that ideas of honour are at the heart of the play, it is equally clear that Falstaff's and Hotspur's behaviour in no way resembles any of the definitions of defective and excessive desire for honour which a wide variety of late sixteenth-century books on honour provide. The *Nicomachean Ethics* provides classical authority for judging the desire for honour excessive, moderate, or defective according to desert.

... Honour may be desired more than is right, or less, or from the right sources and in the right way. We blame both the ambitious man as aiming at honour more than is right and from wrong sources, and the unambitious man as not willing to be honoured even for noble reasons.[2]

This statement of the idea is accepted with no substantial modification by most of the writers on honour of the 1580s and 1590s. Ashley makes it clear that Shakespeare's contemporaries think of a man's 'deservings' as the mark by which he is to be judged ambitious or base minded.[3] 'The ambitious ys blamed because he hunteth after honour ... more greedilie than he ought', Ashley argues, and 'contrariwise the abiect or base minded ys ... reprehended bicause that notwithstanding his good deseruinges he refuseth honour....'[4] This fine line between appropriate and ambitious desire for honour was much considered and carefully defined. Several books or essays written in the decade surrounding Shakespeare's play deal in more or less detail with the question of an excessive desire for honour; they all rely on the basic assumption that honour is a positive good which man has an ethical responsibility to pursue, and that his pursuit of that honour is to be judged excessive or defective according to his deserts. John Norden's *The Mirror of Honor* is within a year of being contemporary with Shakespeare's play, and the danger to true honour which he remarks is typical. 'Among the rest [of the dangers] *Pride* is the most perillous ... whereby ... highest reputation [may be] blemished, and that by assuming more of it selfe to it selfe, then reason or desert will yeeld, from other men'.[5] *The Courtiers Academie* was translated from the Italian in 1598; in it Romei defines honour as 'that ardent heate which enflameth the mind of man to glorious enterprises making him audacious against enemies, and to vices timorous', a Platonic rather than an Aristotelian definition,[6] but consistently justifies only that desire to acquire honour appropriate to the virtuous deed performed.[7] The idea is a commonplace of such books as these. George Whetstone's *The Honorable Reputation of a Souldier*, printed in 1585, and William Segar's *Honor Military and Civil*, printed in 1602, display the consistency with which standard opinion judged a man excessive in his desire for honour only if he sought more honour than he deserved. Whetstone's book praises nineteen illustrious generals, emperors, and kings who, though of mean parentage, were justly elevated to such honourable eminence for valorous and virtuous deeds, but damns the ambitious desire for unjustified honour. In one place, for instance, Whetstone describes the honour due to soldiers who give their lives to protect the state, but he warns against 'the difference between rash and necessary bouldnesse'. Martial virtue consists in doing the state service; 'willful falling upon the enemies sword, is reduculous, daungerous, and very dishonorable'.[8] Segar's book is more a codification of the rules of honourable combat than a definition of the idea, but he expresses the familiar assumption when he bewails the decadent tendency of the aristocratic young to 'glory in the ancient badges, titles, and services of their Auncestors' even though they have done nothing to warrant the honour they claim.[9] Thomas Nashe, in *Christs Teares Over Iervsalem*, condemns as ambition the desire for honour beyond one's – in this case martial – deserts. 'Ambition', Nashe asserts, 'hath changed his name unto honor. . . . Not the honour of the fielde (Ambitions onely enemy) . . . but Brokerly blowne vp honour . . . honour bestowed for damned deserts'.[10]

Certainly if Shakespeare's intent had been to shape his play according to the Aristotelian paradigm which Tillyard and others have proposed, and which has so dominated critical understanding of the play, he would have used the widespread understanding of Aristotelian excess and defect which was available to him. He did not, however, create Hotspur as 'the ambitious man . . . aiming at honour more than is right and from wrong sources', Falstaff as 'the unambitious man . . . not willing to be honoured even for noble reasons', nor make Hal a resolution to those extremes as the man who desires honour 'from the right sources and in the right way'.

Falstaff never rejects reward, merely the established honourable ways of getting it; far from unambitiously declining to be honoured for noble deeds, he, ambitious to a fault, very much wants to be honoured for ignoble deeds. Shakespeare makes the distance between Falstaff's deserts and his desire for reward clear in both the comic and the chronicle scenes. Most explicit are his early exaggerations of the numbers that robbed him and his later demand for reward for killing Hotspur. In the first instance every line he speaks seeks unwarranted acclaim for his presumed swordsmanship and heroism.

> I am a rogue if I were not at half-sword with a dozen of them two hours together. I have scap'd by miracle. I am eight times thrust through the doublet, four through the hose; my buckler cut through

and through; my sword hack'd like a handsaw – ecce signum! I
never dealt better since I was a man. All would not do. A plague of
all cowards!

(II. IV. 154–60)

In the second instance he demands an honourable title on the pretence
of having killed Hotspur.

There is Percy. If your father will do me any honour, so; if not,
let him kill the next Percy himself. I look to be either earl or duke, I
can assure you.

(V. IV. 138–41)

Compared with Falstaff's, Hotspur's desire for honour is modesty
itself, for he quite consciously bases his claim on what he and everyone
else in the play, enemies and allies, consider to be noble deeds. Even
King Henry sees Hotspur's honour as unstained.

A son [Hotspur] who is the theme of honour's tongue,
Amongst a grove, the very straightest plant;
Who is sweet Fortune's minion and her pride. . . .

(I. I. 81–3)

And throughout the play 'honour's tongue' sounds Hotspur's name
again and again. The emphasis is consistently on the honour his valour
deserves, and though Henry will see it as the beginning of rebellion, he
never questions that Hotspur has deserved the 'never dying honour' he
gained 'against renownèd Douglas'.

If Hotspur and Falstaff do not represent Aristotelian moral extremes
for Hal to stand between, clearly the play employs the pervasive theme
of honour in a different manner than has commonly been supposed.
Reference to sixteenth-century books on honour demonstrates a
remarkable similarity between the details of behaviour which they
describe as the perfect attributes of the honourable man and the
behaviour which Shakespeare gives Hotspur. This close and consistent
similarity makes it clear that Hotspur's role in the play is perfectly to
embody the principles of a rigourous and well-defined code of honour;
he is a 'mirror of honour', as many contemporary 'remembrances',
exempla, and biographies of illustrious men used the phrase. Converse-
ly, Shakespeare makes Falstaff consciously and explicitly reject the
code of honour, the demands of which he understands but repudiates;

rather than representing a defective desire for less honour than he deserves, therefore, he dramatizes the nature and consequences of a reasoned rejection of the pervasive code of honour. Shakespeare keeps Hal aloof from the demands of the code, for, rather than accepting or rejecting the code, Hal exploits it for his pragmatic purposes; he is thereby made, much as Shakespeare had done with Bolingbroke in *Richard II*, a mirror of success.

Regarded in this way, the issue of Falstaff's cowardice is moot. At the heart of the code of honour is the principle that honour is more precious than life. The various tracts which elaborately codify the forms of honour to be sought and protected through virtuous deeds virtually all begin with the assumptions that honour originates in martial deeds done in service of the state and that death is to be preferred before the dishonour caused by defeat or flight. 'In any case', Count Romei has Gualinguo remark in *The Courtiers Academie*, 'a man of honor should alwaies preferre death, before infamous saftie. . . .'[11] William Segar, in the preface 'To the Reader' in *The Booke of Honor and Armes* lightly makes the same assumption before he goes on to codify the rules of honourable combat. 'The matter of content is Iustice and Honor. For love whereof, we shun no care of minde, losse of wealth, nor adventure of life'.[12] This position is familiar enough, and, of course, a number of Shakespeare's characters, with varying degrees of sincerity, maintain it. Shakespeare confronts Falstaff with this honourable demand in both the chronicle and comic scenes, and has him consistently and consciously reject it. Falstaff's catechism on honour is in response to Hal's saying, as he exits, that Falstaff 'owest God a death'. 'Well', Falstaff muses, ''tis no matter; honour pricks me on'. But he will have none of the widespread contention, displayed by the books on honour, that honour is more precious than life. It is a merely nominal ethic, and clearly not worth dying for.

What is honour? A word. What is that word honour? Air.

(V. I. 133–4)

'Insensible' to the dead, unavailable to the living, honour is finally for Falstaff 'a mere scutcheon' (V. I. 139). By having Falstaff place such emphasis on honour's belonging uniquely but only ornamentally to the dead, Shakespeare produces a character who is perfectly aware of the central demand which honour makes but who is unwilling to pay the price. Poins has Falstaff exactly, and distinguishes him from his more simply motivated fellows, when he anticipates Falstaff's flight from Gad's Hill.

> Well, for two of them, I know them to be as true-bred cowards as ever turn'd back; and for the third, if he fight longer than he sees reason, I'll forswear arms.
>
> (I. II. 167–9)

At Shrewsbury, Falstaff's actions represent, as do those of the other major characters, precisely the attitude towards honour which he has maintained throughout, and the 'battle' in which he engages there displays the logical conclusion of that attitude. Shakespeare gives Falstaff some very curious things to do at Shrewsbury; none of them further the plot, but the substitution of the bottle of sack for his pistol, the ragamuffin soldiers that Falstaff leads to slaughter, and the battle with Douglas all display a character who by rejecting all the principles of honour has become the antithesis of the honourable man. The ragamuffin soldiers and the sack are convenient instances of Falstaff's satisfying his desire for personal gain and his appetites rather than the demands of honour. As one would expect, the tracts on honour provide evidence that the code considered physical appetites a danger to a soldier's valour, and therefore his honour. Whetstone's *Honorable Reputation of a Souldier*, for instance, remarks that 'When the body is stuffed with delicates, the mind is dull, and desirous of ease, which is the undoer of a Souldier. . . .'[13] One is reminded of the Antony whom Octavius Caesar admired because he, faced with famine, 'didst drink/ The stale of horses and the gilded puddle/ Which beasts would cough at' (I. IV. 61–3). 'And all this', Caesar concludes in comparing the honourable Antony with Cleopatra's Antony, '(It wounds thine honour that I speak it now)/ Was borne so like a soldier that thy cheek/ So much as lank'd not' (I. IV. 68–71). When Hal discovers the bottle of sack in place of Falstaff's pistol we are given a clear if somewhat crude symbol of the deliberate inversion of honourable values which Falstaff represents: he prefers sack, let alone life, before honour. Hal throws the bottle at him and exits; Falstaff replies quite explicitly to this protest at his dishonourable behaviour.

> I like not such grinning honour as Sir Walter hath. Give me life; which if I can save, so; if not, honour comes unlook'd for, and there's an end.
>
> (V. III. 56–9)

Falstaff's counterfeit death is but the logical conclusion of the role he has played in regard to honour, for by escaping from Douglas by feigning death Falstaff is made quite literally to act out his preference for life before honour. Dead, Falstaff could anticipate only the 'mere scutcheon' which honour can provide, and the battle with Douglas provides Falstaff with the opportunity to act upon, and to articulate, his priorities.

> 'Sblood, 'twas time to counterfeit, or that hot termagant Scot had paid me scot and lot too. Counterfeit? I lie; I am no counterfeit. To die is to be a counterfeit; for he is but the counterfeit of a man who hath not the life of a man; but to counterfeit dying when a man thereby liveth, is to be no counterfeit, but the true and perfect image of life indeed.
>
> (V. IV. 112–19)

If Falstaff be the true and perfect image of life, Hotspur is certainly the true and perfect image of honour. Seemingly inconsequential details of Hotspur's behaviour, from the outset of the play, and in each of the eight scenes in which he appears, coincide so exactly with schematic descriptions of the honourable man which had become commonplace in the 1580s and 1590s that there seems little doubt that Shakespeare was at pains to create Hotspur the perfect mirror of honour. This definition of the character represents a consistent modification of the Hotspur who appears in Holinshed. The chronicle characteristically provides the Percys with what little justification for rebellion it allows by reminding its readers that Henry is a usurper 'for the which [usurpation] undoubtedly both he, and his posteritie tasted such troubles, as put them still in daunger of their states, till their direct succeeding line was quite rooted out. . . .'[14] Shakespeare, on the other hand, carefully keeps Hotspur distinct from his fellow rebels by making his act of rebellion – and all his other actions – a consequence of his adherence to the principles of honour.

Hotspur's definition as the honourable man begins with King Henry's demand for the Scottish prisoners and his refusal to ransom Edmund Mortimer. Shakespeare develops the definition from a hint found in Holinshed that the King's demand is counter to the code of honour. Holinshed reports the quarrel, noting that only 'Mordake, Erle of Fife, the Duke of Albanies sonne' had been delivered to the King in spite of the King's having demanded all the prisoners, and concludes by explaining the reason for the Percys' angry response to this demand.

> Wherewith the Percies [were] sore offended, for that they claymed them as their owne proper prisoners, and their peculiar prayes. . . .[15]

The idea that prisoners are a source of honour – the peculiar praise of the captors – and the idea that prisoners, until ransomed, remain the property of their captors unless – as in the case of the Earl of Fife – their royal blood requires their being delivered to the King had been commonplace enough aspects of the code of honour to permit using the ideas on the stage at least as early as *The Spanish Tragedy*. Half of Kyd's second scene, it may be recalled, debates whether Lorenzo or Horatio deserve the honour and reward of Balthazar's capture. The King, appropriately, adjudicates the issue; Hieronimo pleads Horatio's case, 'enforced by nature and by law of arms',[16] and the King awards the ransom and arms to Horatio, the captor, but the noble prisoner to Lorenzo, the Prince. Indeed, Shakespeare returns to the matter of honourable and appropriate disposition of prisoners in the final scene of *1 Henry IV*, so this particular aspect of the codes of honourable behaviour is a familiar enough subjec tfor the stage. A. R. Humphreys notes that 'the law of Arms' permits Hotspur to keep his prisoners, and cites *Pallas Armata* (1683) as authority.[17] He might also have cited William Segar, whose *Honor Military and Civil* details the various rules of honour governing the escape or ransom of prisoners and is more nearly contemporary with the play,[18] though indeed the idea that ransom and other honourable rewards under the law of arms belong to the captor is implicit in most books on the subject. Shakespeare's first scene has King Henry explicitly describe Hotspur's prisoners as 'honourable spoil' and has Westmoreland call Hotspur's victory 'a conquest for a prince to boast of'. It is consequently a clear affront to Hotspur's honour to demand more from him than is the King's due, namely, the royal Earl of Fife, whom Hotspur has appropriately agreed to surrender. Shakespeare further develops that affront by introducing Hotspur's account of the popinjay lord into the quarrel. The emphasis has been on Hotspur's 'well deserved honour', and Hotspur's description of the arduous battle makes clear the distinction between honour 'drearily bought' on the battlefield, as Whetstone's *Honorable Reputation* phrases it,[19] and the foppish posturings of the popinjay.

Shakespeare's introduction of this curious lord also assists in the resolution of the most troublesome problem implicit in his effort to define Hotspur as a mirror of honour. Honour, in both its tangible and intangible forms, is ultimately dispensed by the monarch, and rebellion is, *per se*, a dishonourable act. The popinjay lord provides Hotspur with an honourable excuse for not having delivered his prisoners, and thus delays his open rebellion. He is, of course, still denying the King his prisoners when he describes the popinjay's behaviour to the King, but again Shakespeare has Henry pursue the matter in a manner designed to affront Hotspur's honour without raising the question of his loyalty. When the King describes Hotspur's brother-in-law, as both Shakespeare and the chronicle have it, as 'the foolish Mortimer;/ Who, on my soul, hath willfully betray'd/ The lives of those that he did lead to fight' (I. III. 80–2) the insult is clear. This, after all, is what Falstaff does at Shrewsbury.[20] Hotspur's reply implies no disloyalty to the King; it, rather, defends Mortimer's honour. He has 'drearily bought' his honour in battle with Glendower, and the honour so gained cannot, for Hotspur, exist side by side with the dishonourable treachery of which Mortimer stands accused.

> He never did fall off, my sovereign liege,
> But by the chance of war. To prove that true
> Needs no more but one tongue for all those wounds,
> Those mouthed wounds, which valiantly he took . . .
> In changing hardiment with great Glendower. . . .
> Then let not him be slandered with revolt.
>
> (I. III. 94–112)

The King does not argue. He answers Hotspur with a deliberate insult, accusing him of lying and dismissing him with a belittling form of address.

> Thou dost belie him, Percy, thou dost belie him. . . .
> Art thou not asham'd? But, sirrah, henceforth
> Let me not hear you speak of Mortimer.
> Send me your prisoners with the speediest means,
> Or you shall hear in such a kind from me
> As will displease you.
>
> (I. III, 113–22)

It is this affront which arouses Hotspur's celebrated ire, but this is a quite appropriate, not an excessive, response for the honourable man to make. The speech in which Hotspur thinks 'it were an easy leap/ To pluck bright honour from the pale-fac'd moon' is set in a scene which displays Hotspur's irascibility, not his ambition, and sixteenth-century books on honour usually associate anger with honour. This is probably the speech which most occasioned the quasi-Aristotelian reading of the play, but if the urge to see the play as being organized according to a specific philosophical scheme remains overpowering, the Platonic description of man's tripartite soul provides a considerably more satisfactory explanation of Hotspur's outburst – and of Falstaff's sensuality – than does the Aristotelian ethic. In the fourth book of *The Republic*, Plato identifies the desire for honour with 'passion or spirit', which combines with the rational and the concupiscent to make up the three principles of the soul. This identification is expressed in the sixteenth century in various places; Robert Ashley is again the most explicit.

And seeing (as *Plato* will haue yt) the powre of the mind ys of three partes, whereof one ys named reason, another termed anger, and a third called desire. . . . Honour seemeth to haue his root and beginning of the second, for . . . the desire of honour . . . as *Plato* saieth, cometh out of the angry part of the mind. . . . So we see that men of great mindes are much moved with honour, but that the abiect and baser sort be nothing affected therwith because the sence and feeling thereof ys geuen only to those that are of high spirite.[21]

This connection between the irascible passion and the desire for honour is a more likely origin than the theory of Aristotelian excess provides of Hotspur's outburst in Act I – just as the Platonic idea that concupiscence uncontrolled by reason turns to sloth is a more likely origin of Falstaff's behaviour. One has only to recall Pyrocles' ire in Canto 5 and Cymocles' sloth in Canto 6 of Book II of *The Faerie Queene* to observe a more explicitly allegorical use of the Paltonic idea. By having Hotspur respond with this angry outburst to the affronts Henry has levelled against his honour, Shakespeare continues to define Hotspur as a man who perfectly embodies all the characteristics of the honourable man.

The dilemma remains that it is the King who has affronted Hotspur's honour, and disloyalty to the king is itself a source of dishonour. Hotspur, after all, has just asked that Mortimer not 'be slandered with revolt'. At the next moment in the play, after King Henry's insult and Hotspur's angry response have been displayed, Shakespeare has Worcester and Northumberland quite illogically tell Hotspur, as though he were ignorant of the fact, that Mortimer had been proclaimed heir to the throne by Richard. This delayed information provides a resolution to the dilemma, even if it be realistically improbable that Hotspur would not know of Mortimer's claim, for Hotspur can now see his virtuous and therefore honourable duty to be the restoration of Mortimer as the rightful king. The long speech that he is given in response to this information emphasizes the injustice of which his father and uncle have been guilty by aiding Bolingbroke and the honour which they have consequently lost.

> Shall it for shame be spoken in these days,
> Or fill up chronicles in time to come,
> That men of your ability and power
> Did gage them both in an unjust behalf
> (As both of you, God pardon it! have done)
> To put down Richard, that sweet lovely rose,
> And plant this thorn, this canker, Bolingbroke?
>
> (I. III. 170–6)

This justification is as much a part of Hotspur's honourable behaviour as his anger, for Hotspur is consistently made a mirror of the orthodox, Aristotelian sort of honour, which is always defined as the reward of virtue. By providing this justification, Shakespeare allows Hotspur to pursue his honour by righting the wrong which he considers Bolingbroke, with Percy's aid, to have committed.

> ... Yet time serves wherein you may redeem
> Your banish'd honours and restore yourselves
> Into the good thoughts of the world again;
> Revenge the jeering and disdain'd contempt
> Of this proud king. ...
>
> (I. III. 180–4)

Restoring their tarnished honour is never, of course, Northumberland's or Worcester's motive. They, rather, are concerned to protect themselves against the King who they know will find 'a time to pay us home'. Hotspur's commitment to the principles of honour isolates him from the pragmatic workings of his allies – and of his enemies, a naïveté which will have disastrous consequences for him at Shrewsbury.

In the first of the scenes at Shrewsbury Shakespeare develops a virtually self-contained dramatic pattern which reflects in small both the nobility and the practical shortcomings of Hotspur's commitment to honour. He enters with Douglas, who calls him 'the king of honour', to discover that Northumberland's forces will not arrive. Holinshed had indeed reported wholesale defections from the rebel's cause, and Shakespeare dramatizes these defections as the occasion of a series of choices which Hotspur must make. He responds to the first news in practical fashion; he knows that his father's absence weakens their army, but argues that they now have a refuge should fortune turn against them. 'Were it good', he asks, 'To set the exact wealth of all our states/ All at one cast?' (IV. i. 45–7). But Shakespeare has Worcester argue that Northumberland's absence might 'breed a kind of question in our cause./ ... We of the off'ring side', he argues, 'Must keep aloof from strict arbitrement,/ And stop all sight-holes, every loop from whence/ The eye of reason may pry in upon us' (IV. i. 68–72). This slur on the justice of their cause touches Hotspur's ruling concern, and Shakespeare gives him a characteristic reply. Northumberland's absence, for Hotspur, now 'lends a lustre and more great opinion,/ A larger dare to our great enterprise ...' (IV. i. 77–8). Vernon enters to this with his glittering description of the King's forces and of the renascent Prince of Wales, news which fills Hotspur with eager expectation of the honourable actions of war, the same sort of eager irascibility Shakespeare had him display in his response to the King's insult in Act I.

> They come like sacrifices in their trim,
> And to the fire-ey'd maid of smoky war
> All hot and bleeding will we offer them.
>   ... I am on fire
> To hear this rich reprisal is so nigh,
> And not yet ours.
>
> (IV. i. 113–19)

Shakespeare delays Vernon's other news, Glendower's absence, until after Hotspur's compelling desire for honour has been thus brought forward, by which time no deterrent of a merely practical kind can

47

compete. The scene had begun with Hotspur's debating the effect on the rebellion of Northumberland's sickness; it concludes with Hotspur so committed to honour that he can happily dismiss success – and life – to serve it.

Doomsday is near. Die all, die merrily.

(IV. i. 134)

Yet this compulsion is but part of the perfect image of honour, corresponding to Hotspur's outburst in I. iii. There Shakespeare had Hotspur justify his opposition to the King by describing it as a virtuous and therefore honourable effort to restore Mortimer; he re-introduces that justification into the play in Hotspur's next scene. After a brief scene which introduces Falstaff's pitiful soldiers, the action returns to the rebel camp to disclose a Hotspur who, though eager for battle, is prepared by the end of the scene to send his uncle to negotiate with the King. Much of this scene is taken up by a long speech which Shakespeare gives Hotspur to rehearse the Percy's role in Bolingbroke's usurpation and the dishonour they have consequently suffered.

In short time after, he depos'd the King,
Soon after that depriv'd him of his life. . . .
To make that worse, suff'red his kinsman March
(Who is, if every owner were well plac'd,
Indeed his king) to be engag'd in Wales . . .
Disgrac'd me in my happy victories . . .
Rated mine uncle from the Council board;
In rage dismiss'd my father from the court . . .
And in conclusion drove us to seek out
This head of safety. . . .

(IV. iii. 90–103)

No narrative or expository purpose is served by this rehearsal, for the information it provides is already common property. It does, however, provide the necessary balance to Hotspur's honour. In his prior scene, Hotspur's honourable impatience for the glories of battle was empha-sized; here his sense of the virtuous intent which justifies his actions and of the dishonour the King has offered him are the central concerns. Hotspur's offer to negotiate a settlement thus balances the grandiose 'Die all, die merrily' with which Shakespeare had concluded the previous scene. At the end of the next scene in which Hotspur appears

48

these two aspects of his honour are merged in a single speech. After further characterizing Hotspur by having Worcester assume that he would abandon the war should 'the liberal and kind offer of the King' be made known to him, Shakespeare gives Hotspur a speech which precisely states the balance between his eager pursuit of honour and his justification of that pursuit.

> O gentlemen, the time of life is short!
> To spend that shortness basely were too long
> If life did ride upon a dial's point,
> Still ending at the arrival of an hour.
> And if we live, we live to tread on kings;
> If die, brave death, when princes die with us!
> Now for our consciences, the arms are fair,
> When the intent of bearing them is just.
>
> (V. II. 81–8)

Hotspur thus enters battle the picture of an honourable man, secure in conscience and indifferent to death if it provide honour to an otherwise valueless life. His death is displayed as the logical consequence of this attitude. Hotspur, wishing that Hal's 'name in arms were now as great as mine', only regrets that Hal is not a more honourable foe, and his death, immediately juxtaposed with Falstaff's feigning death, is as precisely the true and perfect image of honour as Falstaff's action is the image of life. He dies pronouncing the basic article of the creed of honour.

> I better brook the loss of brittle life
> Than those proud titles thou hast won of me.
> They wound my thoughts worse than thy sword my flesh.
>
> (V. IV. 78–80)

As Shrewsbury is the scene where Shakespeare brings Hotspur and Falstaff to the conclusions demanded by the roles in the theme of honour he has given them to play, so it displays the successful consequences of Hal's role. Hal, throughout the play, is kept aloof from the intricate demands of honour that so compel Hotspur and repel Falstaff; Shakespeare makes Hal concerned with honour only as a means to other ends. Hal had sounded the theme of honour in his first soliloquy, which, if viewed in terms of the code of honour, is more devious than the 'Aristotelian' reading of the play assumes. That soliloquy, the interview with his father in Act III, and his actions at Shrewsbury comprise Hal's explicit part in the theme of honour, though some comic commentary on the theme may be intended by the scenes at Gad's Hill and The Boar's Head. Hal's part in the theme of honour is, then, conspicuously less extensive than Hotspur's, and though Shakespeare uses extra-narrative scenes such as Hotspur's conversation with Kate and argument with Glendower to expand the idea of Hotspur's commitment to honour, he consistently displays Hal in the comic scenes as indifferent to or, even, amused by the sort of honour which Hotspur so thoroughly serves. Success is Hal's motive, and he differs from Hotspur and Falstaff in his capacity to use honour as a means to that success.

Hal's first soliloquy announces his attitude towards honour; he intends, by engaging in low behaviour, to delay the acquisition of honour so that, when acquired, his reputation will seem grander than it otherwise would. The soliloquy is familiar, but attention to its metaphoric and literal statements that reputation is but a façade that can be advantageously enhanced demonstrates it to be a thoroughly pragmatic plan to exploit apparent dishonour for advantage, rather than a statement of a sort of nascent nobility awaiting education or maturity. The images all emphasize the effects of unexpected behaviour on observers; Hal nowhere considers the inherent worth of the behaviour he plans.

> So, when this loose behaviour I throw off
> And pay the debt I never promised,
> By how much better than my word I am,
> By so much shall I falsify men's hopes;
> And like bright metal on a sullen ground,
> My reformation, glitt'ring o'er my fault,
> Shall show more goodly, and attract more eyes
> Than that which hath no foil to set it off.
> I'll so offend, to make offence a skill,
> Redeeming time when men think least I will.

(I. ii. 192–201)

This attitude towards honour differs from Hotspur's in its intention to exploit rather than serve the code of honour. Hal sees an honourable reputation as a useful political commodity, rather than seeing honour as an ideal to which life itself must be sacrificed, and he intends to exploit appearances to increase his grip on that commodity. To comprehend the difference between this attitude and the one Shakespeare gives Hotspur, one only need realize that most of the books on honour considered it so demanding a code that they argue that a single dishonourable act irrevocably destroys one's honour. *The Courtiers Academie* addresses itself to the problem with a typical judgment.

> ... The greater sort of men hold their honor so deare, as that they dare not do evill, for feare of the losse thereof, knowing that it once only being lost, can never be recovered.[22]

Nor is the company one keeps to be taken light-heartedly by the man bent on honour. James Cleland's advice to his student reader describes 'with what company [they] should converse'.

> Companie changeth mens manners. ... Hee that keepeth company with the wicked shal hardly escape without blemish, either in life or credite.[23]

Certainly the jealous and constant protection of honour is a familiar enough characteristic among noble figures of the Elizabethan stage for this manipulation of it to be marked in Hal. This first soliloquy introduces to the audience a unique character who, though no malignant Machiavel, intends to exploit appearances to gain success.

Hal's interview with his father develops the plan. As Falstaff will serve as a contrast, so Hotspur will serve as a means to the reputation Hal intends to acquire. It is an unusual scene. After a series of scenes filled with Hotspur's honourable outbursts or with rapid, witty, and irreverent dialogue between Falstaff and Hal, this stands alone with its long, discursive speeches analysing the nature of and prophesying the effects of Hal's behaviour. Save for the single, if major, fact that Henry can after this count Hal as a trusted ally, the scene contributes nothing to the narrative. It is clearly a pause, put right at the centre of the play, designed to unfold the basic characterization of Hal which his first soliloquy had implied.

Hal is first and last his father's son, for, though Shakespeare here keeps Henry IV from recognizing the fact, they share the same assumptions and aspirations. Henry has two kinds of complaints about Hal's behaviour, and the fact that the first is dealt with perfunctorily and the second at detailed length further defines the sort of response which Shakespeare gives Hal to the code of honour. Henry first finds it incomprehensible, unless Hal be divinely sent to punish him, that Hal should match the 'greatness of [his] blood' (III. ii. 16) with 'such inordinate and low desires' (III. ii. 12). Hal, discrediting the excessive reports that 'base newsmongers' have brought to Henry's ear, admits to the faults of youth and asks forgiveness. They are speaking the language of honour, for throughout sixteenth-century discussions of the idea runs the assumption that those of high birth have a correspondingly greater responsibility to be honourable. Castiglione's *Courtier* is one example.

> For it is a great deale less dispraise for him that is not born a gentleman to faile in the acts of vertue, then for a gentleman. If he swerve from the steps of his ancestors, hee staineth the name of his family.[24]

In Count Romei's *Academie*, also, the Signior Gualinguo who begins the discourse on honour by distinguishing between 'honor Naturall', and 'acquired honor', defines the former as that which man 'bringeth ... from his mother's wombe, and preserveth ... unspotted, except through some greevous offence or suspition, he loose this good opinion'.[25] William Segar sounds the same note.

> And the more highlie he be borne, the worse reputation he meriteth, if he cannot continue the honor left him by his Ancestors.[26]

Shakespeare gives only thirty lines to Henry's concern about and Hal's apology for having ignored these basic demands of honour. Hal asks forgiveness, and Shakespeare has Henry dismiss the issue with a brief 'God pardon thee!' before he turns the scene to its central concern with the practical effects of Hal's action, a concern which will occupy the next 130 lines.

Henry complains that Hal's actions have ruined 'The hope and expectation of thy time' (III. ii. 36), and quite unabashedly asserts that the manipulation of public reputation is necessary to success. As in Hal's first soliloquy, the terms in which Shakespeare has the Lancasters express themselves emphasize their assumption that honour is a useful façade which may be put on or off, like masks, at will. Hal had there determined that his reformation should 'show more goodly and attract more eyes/ Than that which hath no foil to set it off'. Henry here describes the effects of having 'dressed' himself in humility.

And then I stole all courtesy from heaven,
And dress'd myself in such humility
That I did pluck allegiance from men's hearts,
Loud shouts and salutations from their mouths
Even in the presence of the crowned King.
Thus did I keep my person fresh and new,
My presence, like a robe pontifical,
Ne'er seen but wond'red at; and so my state,
Seldom but sumptuous, showed like a feast. . . .

(III. II. 50–8)

Conspicuously absent from this is any sense that an honourable reputation, being the mark of virtuous action, is valuable in itself, an attitude Hotspur is consistently made to exemplify. And when Henry turns to comparisons between Hal and King Richard, as he then was, and between Hotspur and himself, as the young Bolingbroke, his description of honour as a means to political ends becomes more extreme. Richard lost the crown because he did not attend to his reputation, Henry asserts, and he warns that Hal stands in similar danger. Hotspur, Henry most illogically asserts, has more right to the crown than Hal, for he has achieved a more honourable reputation. This last is at once the most extreme conclusion of Henry's attitude towards the practical political effects of an honourable reputation and the clearest instance of the difference between Hotspur's thorough-going commitment to the ideals of honour and the Lancasters' exploitation of those ideas.

Now, by my sceptre, and my soul to boot,
He hath more worthy interest to the state
Than thou, the shadow of succession;
For of no right, nor colour like to right,
He doth fill fields with harness in the realm,
Turns head against the lion's armed jaws,
And, being no more in debt to years than thou,
Leads ancient lords and reverend bishops on
To bloody battles and to bruising arms.

(III. II. 97–105)

Shakespeare delays Hal's response until all of Henry's accusations have been expressed, then in that response gives Hal precisely the same assumptions about the nature of honour. There are alternative responses. The King had concluded by accusing Hal of being able 'To fight against me under Percy's pay .../ To show how much thou art degenerate' (III. II. 126–8), so were honour at the stake it would be logical for Hal to profess his interest in maintaining the succession in order to avert civil discord, or his interest in putting down rebellion, or some other manifestly virtuous interest. Indeed, in the sources from which the play is drawn, just such an interest is the Prince's motive. In Holinshed and in *The Famous Victories* this meeting is used by the Prince to convince his father that he has no intention of usurping the throne, which suspicion Holinshed reports slanderous informants to have planted in the King. In the play, however, Shakespeare modifies the scene to accord with his plan to develop Hal as the pragmatist who, aware of other men's commitment to the code of honour, determines that exploitation of that commitment is the way to success. Consequently, Shakespeare has Hal respond to Henry's complaints by announcing his intention to use Hotspur's reputation for his own gain.

> I will redeem all this on Percy's head
> And, in the closing of some glorious day,
> Be bold to tell you that I am your son,
> When I will wear a garment all of blood,
> And stain my favours in a bloody mask,
> Which, wash'd away, shall scour my shame with it.
>
> (III. II. 132–7)

This is precisely the intention Hal had announced in his first soliloquy, and it is an intention which remains fundamentally different from the sort of commitment to honour which controls Hotspur. Hotspur's honourable reputation is useful to Hal, and he means to acquire it.

Hal's first speech at Shrewsbury puts into action his long-anticipated bid to enter the lists of chivalry. The reasons he gives for challenging Hotspur to single combat are beneficent and humane, and there is no evidence that the play intends that he be cynically or ironically understood. That Hal is pragmatic does not mean that he is diabolic. In fact, however, the action demands Shrewsbury, not a single encounter between Hal and Hotspur, so Hal's offer can only be seen as a definition of character, not a potential alternative to the narrative line. Hal had planned to make Hotspur exchange 'His glorious deeds for my indignities', and Shakespeare appropriately dramatizes that plan by having Hal challenge Hotspur to a trial of arms, the most explicitly honourable act available, to mark Hal's first step in this successful acquisition of an honourable reputation. The effect of this step is quickly seen in Vernon's glowing report to the rebel camp of Hal's challenge. Hotspur, jealous of his honour, asks if the challenge 'seemed ... in contempt', and Vernon does considerably more than reassure him. His account describes a model instance of that honourable balance between the offering of honest praise and the rejection of self-praise which Glendower had so contorted in his argument with Hotspur and which Hotspur and Douglas so carefully maintain.

> No, by my soul. I never in my life
> Did hear a challenge urg'd more modestly. . . .
> He gave you all the duties of a man . . .
> Spoke your deservings like a chronicle;
> Making you even better than his praise
> By still dispraising praise valued with you;
> And, which became him like a prince indeed,
> He made a blushing cital of himself. . . .
>
> (V. II. 51–61)

This and Vernon's other descriptions exaggerate what the audience has already seen, and so exhibit the first successful consequence of Hal's deliberate entry into the honourable life. His plan is succeeding, for as first described in Vernon's speech his new reputation does in fact 'show more goodly .../ Than that which hath no foil to set it off'. Vernon, who had described Hal, armed, as having risen from the ground 'like feathered Mercury' and who has heard Hal's challenge, explicitly draws the comparison between these things and Hal's earlier behaviour.

> . . . But let me tell the world,
> If he outlive the envy of this day,
> England did never owe so sweet a hope,
> So much misconstrued in his wantonness.
>
> (V. II. 65–8)

Hal's victory over Hotspur, with Falstaff lying by feigning death, puts into action the success which Hal had planned and Vernon described. It also dramatizes Hal's essential indifference to honour except as a means to other ends. The epitaph which Hal speaks over Hotspur's body is as much a farewell to the ideals of honour which had so compelled Hotspur's behaviour as to Hotspur himself. John Dover Wilson compares Hal's supposed epitaph over Falstaff with Hamlet's over Yorick,[27] but Hal's speech over the dead Hotspur bears even closer resemblance with Hamlet's tracing the noble dust of Alexander until he finds it stopping a bung-hole. Hamlet's trials in that play lead more logically to his rejection of human glory and honour as vanity, so in Hal's mouth, by comparison, the speech seems largely a commonplace, but it is consistent with, and may even be a belated effort to provide a moral basis for, Hal's indifference to honour as an ideal.

> *Hotspur.* . . . Percy, thou art dust,
>   And food for —
> *Hal.* For worms, brave Percy. Fare thee well,
>   great heart!
> Ill-weav'd ambition, how much art thou shrunk!
> When that this body did contain a spirit,
> A kingdom for it was too small a bound;
> But now two paces of the vilest earth
> Is room enough.

(V. iv. 84–91)

The Hal who then meets Falstaff with a willingness to gild a lie 'with the happiest terms I have' and who elaborately arranges for the honourable release of Douglas is not a different or more educated Hal than the Hal of Act I, nor is he an embodiment of the triumph of moral mediocrity; he is a character in whom is dramatized the successful consequences of the pragmatic plans he was made to articulate in his first soliloquy and develop in his interview with King Henry. There is in the play no outright condemnation of this pragmatism, and if Hal's response to the world of the play makes him less sensual than Falstaff, less honourable than Hotspur, and less engaging than either, it is the response which, by definition, brings him success.

The structure suggested by the present argument is more characteristically Shakespearian than the supposed Aristotelian paradigm. To dramatize the beginnings of England's civil wars, Shakespeare makes honour a code of behaviour central to the play and gives each of the major characters a different response to the demands of that code. Each suffers or enjoys the logical and ethical consequences of his response. Hamlet will, in a few years, call for plays 'to hold . . . the mirror up to nature; to show virtue her own feature, scorn her own image, and the very age and body of the time his form and pressure' (III. II. 20–3). The three principals of *1 Henry IV*, and the play itself, are such mirrors.

Notes to Chapter 2

[1] David Berkeley and Donald Eidson, 'The Theme of *Henry IV, Part 1*', *Shakespeare Quarterly* XIX (1968) pp. 25–31, provide the most recent study. They consider honour only 'a prominent subtheme' (p. 25), but in that context agree with the customary interpretation. They cite as proponents of this interpretation Zeeveld, *Shakespeare Quarterly* III (1952); Haydn, *The Counter-Renaissance* (New York, 1950); Boas, *Shakespeare and his Predecessors* (New York, 1896); and W. B. Hunter, 'Falstaff', *South Atlantic Quarterly* L (1951), pp. 86–95 (through error Hunter's article is cited as appearing in *Shakespeare Quarterly*). Hunter, indeed, extends this Aristotelian scheme to assign to the Prince the virtues of 'liberality', 'good temper', 'temperance', 'a sense of humor', and, even, 'magnanimity', comparing these with appropriate excesses and defects in Hotspur and Falstaff. Curiously, Berkeley and Eidson overlook Tillyard's formulation of this interpretation in *Shakespeare's History Plays* (1944). Cleanth Brooks and Robert Heilman further sanction the idea and give it wide distribution in their text, *Understanding Drama* (New York, 1948). A clear indication of the fairly recent but pervasive acceptance of the idea may be gained by comparing Kittredge's introduction to the play (Ginn & Co., 1940), where no hint of the 'Aristotelian' reading of the play is implied, with Ribner's introduction to the play in his revision of the Kittredge edition, where Ribner easily assumes that 'in defining true courage and honour, Shakespeare adopts the Aristotelian principle of temperance, with real virtue as a mean between extremes' (p. 756).

[2] Aristotle, *Nicomachean Ethics*, IV.4 in *The Works of Aristotle*, tr. W. D. Ross (Oxford, 1925), Vol. IX.

[3] Watson consistently assumes that 'Aristotle's original definitions are a hidden spring from which flow most of the ideas [about honour] of the writers of the sixteenth century' (p. 66). He nowhere takes notice, however, of this shared emphasis on desert as the measure of excess and defect; since he is, in any case, not concerned with Shakespeare's development of the idea of honour in individual plays, Watson makes only a passing reference to *1 Henry IV*.

[4] Ashley, p. 41.

[5] John Norden, *The Mirror of Honor* (London, 1597), p. 22.

[6] See below p. 45.

[7] Romei, p. 78.

[8] George Whetstone, *The Honorable Reputation of a Souldier* (London, 1585), sig. E.

[9] William Segar, *Honor Military and Civil* (London, 1602), p. 203.

[10] Thomas Nashe, *Christs Teares Over Iervsalem*, in *The Works of Thomas Nashe*, ed. Ronald B. McKerrow (Oxford, 1958), II, 82.

[11] Romei, p. 101. Watson, in his effort to disjoin the ethics of 'pagan humanism' and Christianity, argues that *The Courtiers Academie* is here presenting 'the Stoic justification of suicide'. Gualinguo, the spokesman, does conclude that 'upon this foundation the Stoikes in some cases permitted the violent killing of one's selfe to avoide a dishonorable life', but the whole argument is intended to emphasize the power that honour has always held rather than to justify suicide in spite of Christian prohibition. Watson does, however, cite several other instances where the assumption that honour is more precious than life is expressed (pp. 157, 215, 217, 219, and 361).

[12] William Segar, *The Booke of Honor and Armes* (London, 1590), sig. A2.

[13] Whetstone, sig. Dii.

[14] Raphael Holinshed, *The Last Volume of the Chronicles of England, Scotlande, and Irelande . . .* (London, 1577), p. 1138.

[15] Holinshed, p. 1136. The *OED* lists *prayes* as a sixteenth-century variant spelling of *praise* and provides a definition appropriate here: 'That for which a person . . . is, or deserves to be, praised.' The second edition of Holinshed (1587) substitutes *preies* for *prayes*. *Preies* is not among the variants listed for *praise*, but is one form of *prize* or *price*. This may be the meaning conveyed by the second edition.

[16] Thomas Kyd, *The Spanish Tragedy*, ed. J. R. Malryne (New Mermaids Series, London, 1970), I.ii.168.

[17] A. R. Humphreys, ed. *Henry IV, Part 1* (Arden Shakespeare Series, London, 1961), p. 8, n. to ll. 91–4. Humphreys further remarks that Holinshed does not mention Hotspur's justification under the law of arms. However, Humphreys uses the 1807–8 reprint of the second edition (1587) of Holinshed for his editorial purposes, which edition does not retain Holinshed's original description of the Percys' claiming the prisoners as 'their peculiar prayes' (see n. 15 above).

[18] *Honor Military and Civil*, Bk. 1, Chs. 31–2, *passim*.

[19] Whetstone, sig. Bv.

[20] See Humphreys note to V.iii.36 (Falstaff's confession that he led his soldiers 'where they are peppered') for reference to various sixteenth- and seventeenth-century statements which condemn betrayal by a commander of his men as particularly dishonourable.

21 Ashley, p. 40.

22 Romei, sig. P2.

23 James Cleland, *The Institution of a Young Noble Man* (Oxford, 1607), pp. 191–2.

24 Castiglione, pp. 31–2.

25 Romei, sig. Liv.

26 *The Booke of Honor and Armes*, sig. F1–F2.

27 John Dover Wilson, *The Fortunes of Falstaff* (Cambridge, 1943), pp. 67–8.

Chapter 3

JULIUS CAESAR
The Honourable Brutus

The consistent habit of mind which caused Elizabethans to think of political or other public forms of behaviour in terms of honour is apparent in Shakespeare's dramatization of the assassination of Julius Caesar. Rather than organizing the play as a series of conflicts between honour and other motives for behaviour, however, as he had done with *1 Henry IV*, Shakespeare provides the play with its unity, and incidentally foreshadows the form of the later tragedies, by making the source of Brutus's grandeur the ironic and inevitable source of his tragedy. The noble Brutus' petty squabbling with Cassius in Act IV and his pathetic search for someone worthy enough to hold the sword on which he means to die in Act V are but the logical consequences of the idealistic assumptions about honour with which Shakespeare provides Brutus early in the play. Seeing Brutus as a consistent tragic hero is for this reason crucial to understanding Shakespeare's intent. Plutarch's various retellings of the story serve the purposes of moral biography. Dante's placing Brutus and Cassius in two of the mouths of Dis parallels their sin against earthly order with Judas' against heavenly. Shakespeare gives form to his play by concentrating on the honourable motives and the consequent tragedy of the chief assassin. Examination of Shakespeare's treatment of Brutus as a man who suffers from a dilemma implicit in the ideal of honour to which he adheres provides ample evidence that the play's unity is as rigorous, and results from much the same dramatic form, as the unity of *Othello* or *Macbeth*.

In his first dialogue with Cassius, some 160 lines into the play, Brutus states his creed.

What is it that you would impart to me?
If it be aught toward the general good,

Set honour in one eye and death i' th' other,
And I will look on both indifferently;
For let the gods so speed me as I love
The name of honour more than I fear death.

(I. II. 84–9)

This introduces the basic paradox in Brutus' motive. He is so firmly committed to honour that although typically, for a sixteenth-century man of honour, prepared to risk death for its sake , he also assumes that his honourable instincts will inevitably enable him to serve 'the general good'. Shakespeare thus introduces into the play an idea of honour quite distinct from the orthodox, Aristotelian formulation, for Brutus' assumption that his honour is rather an inherent guide to proper behaviour in a decadent world than a reward he gains for virtuous action makes him an entirely different kind of man of honour than, for example, Hotspur. The *OED* defines this sort of honour as 'a fine sense of and strict allegiance to what is due or right'. It is the aberrant sort of honour described above, in Chapter I, as usually appearing in those sixteenth-century speculations about honour which assume that a world in moral decay requires such a standard of behaviour.[1] That Brutus is never made to question the validity of his honourable instincts as a guide to the general welfare of Rome provides the basic and tragic irony of the play. Shakespeare creates a world around Brutus which supports his sense of honour by pressing him to act according to his honourable instincts, seen as the only valid standard left in an otherwise topsy-turvy world where Roman triumphs over Roman and the spectre of kingship has again appeared. Brutus' commitment to honour is thereby made more compelling, and Shakespeare has him unquestioningly obey his sense of honour even in the face of such other compelling demands as political authority, reason, and friendship make.

Shakespeare develops their first dialogue by having Cassius respond to Brutus' asserted love of 'the name of honour' with arguments that are irrelevant to or even antithetical to 'the general good'. 'Well, honour is the subject of my story', Cassius maintains, and proceeds to demonstrate, with two examples, that Caesar has neither the physical strength nor the courage to warrant his exalted position. His argument is conspicuously not concerned with 'the general good', but rather with the dishonour which other men suffer in comparison with Caesar's

E

eminence. Shakespeare gives Brutus comparatively little to say during this dialogue, but his few lines do indicate that Cassius' dwelling on the 'name of honour' rather than on 'the general good' has its effect. Brutus' response to the first off-stage shout had displayed concern over the issue of kingship.

> What means this shouting? I do fear the people
> Choose Caesar for their king.
>
> (I. II. 79–80)

In the midst of Cassius' argument, some fifty lines later, he believes that the second shout is 'For some new honours that are heap'd on Caesar' (I. II. 134). This is a more petty, or at least a more personal, response, and Shakespeare has Cassius continue by referring openly to the danger Brutus' honour suffers from Caesar's eminence.

> Why, man, he doth bestride the narrow world
> Like a Colossus, and we petty men
> Walk under his huge legs and peep about
> To find ourselves dishonourable graves. . . .
> 'Brutus' and 'Caesar'. What should be in that 'Caesar'?
> Why should that name be sounded more than yours?
> Write them together: yours is as fair a name.
> Sound them: it doth become the mouth as well.
> Weigh them: it is as heavy. Conjure with 'em:
> 'Brutus' will start a spirit as soon as 'Caesar'.
>
> (I. II. 135–47)

Cassius has thus directed Brutus' love of the name of honour towards an entirely different end than Brutus initially asserted that it served. Saying nothing towards the general good, Cassius puts Brutus' honour in one eye and Caesar's in the other and bids Brutus observe his own eclipse. By having Brutus succumb to Cassius' argument that he must compete with Caesar for 'the name of honour', Shakespeare creates a perspective in which the audience can begin to view sceptically Brutus' absolute assumption that his sense of honour is a valid guide to actions beneficial to Rome. Brutus is never aware of this paradoxical mixture, and in Cassius' soliloquy, which concludes this expository scene, Shakespeare defines Brutus' dilemma precisely. Cassius knows Brutus to be 'noble', but has discovered that his 'honourable mettle may be wrought/ From that it is dispos'd' (I. II. 306–7). Continued success will depend on exploiting Brutus' love of the name of honour.

> I will this night,
> In several hands, in at his windows throw,
> As if they came from several citizens,
> Writings, all tending to the great opinion
> That Rome holds of his name; wherein obscurely
> Caesar's ambition shall be glanced at.
>
> (I. II. 312–17)

At the beginning of Act II Shakespeare dramatizes Brutus' decision to kill Caesar. One minute, at most, before this scene begins the audience hears Casca make some very curious remarks about virtue and vice.

> O, he [Brutus] sits high in all the people's hearts;
> And that which would appear offence in us,
> His countenance, like richest alchemy,
> Will change to virtue and to worthiness.
>
> (I. III. 157–60)

Casca does not mean that Brutus' participation will make their deed merely seem virtuous, but, as the alchemical metaphor suggests, that his honourable reputation will actually transmute their offence from vice to virtue. Shakespeare thus has Casca absolutely reverse the Aristotelian definition by having him assume that if an action be honourable, or done by an honourable man, then it must, *per se*, be virtuous. This is a decadent and perverse reversal, and Brutus' decision to kill Caesar is made in this encouraging context. In his first soliloquy, whether illogically or not,[2] Brutus states his decision to kill Caesar in the most idealistic of terms; he, indeed, is prepared to ignore his friendship and personal admiration of Caesar to prevent what he sees as a danger to the general welfare. But Shakespeare also makes the decision partly a result of Cassius' successful appeal to Brutus' sense of honour, and so produces the familiar enigma. Brutus knows 'no personal cause to spurn at him,/ But for the general' (II. I. 11–12), but, as Shakespeare reminds us, Brutus has also seen Cassius' mock 'Writings, all tending to the great opinion/ That Rome holds of his name' (I. II. 314–15). His idealistic opposition to supposed tyranny and his absolute dependence on his own sense of what honour demands are inextricably mixed at this climactic moment of the play. Brutus, here as throughout, thinks the removal of Caesar an honourable act, but the audience has already been made suspicious of that honour, and Shakespeare hastens to display a variety of instances in which honour is practised for its own sake, rather than for the general good.

The three commands which Brutus delivers to the conspirators immediately after his decision for assassination display the first stages of his delusion, and Shakespeare makes Brutus' honourable instinct the motive for each command. Plutarch marvels that the conspirators, though they took no oath, kept the plot secret; Shakespeare has Brutus assume that swearing an oath would be an act which would 'stain/ The even virtue of our enterprise' (II. 1. 132–3). Plutarch records that all the conspirators omitted Cicero because he was a coward; Shakespeare first has Metellus Cimber suggest that Cicero's presence would lend the conspiracy the same sort of honourable prestige that Brutus provides, then has Brutus protect his own pre-eminence – with a response irrelevant to any concern for 'the general good' – by arguing that Cicero 'will never follow anything/ That other men begin' (II. 1. 151–2).[3] No harm comes to the conspiracy as a consequence of these two commands, and they are clearly not required by the narrative. They stand as the first full demonstration on stage of the Brutus whose every decision is made by reference to his inherent sense of what is honourable. A good deal of harm results from the third command. Plutarch's account of Brutus' persuading the other conspirators not to kill Antonius follows his account of the assassination, and he has Brutus argue, first, that killing Antonius would not be 'honest' and, further, that 'Antonius, being a noble-minded and courageous man', would after Caesar's death 'willingly help his country to recover her liberty, having [the conspirators] an example unto him to follow their courage and virtue'.[4] Shakespeare uses the occasion to show us a Brutus who avoids killing Antony lest their deed take on characteristics incompatible with his honourable preconception of it.

> Let's be sacrificers, but not butchers, Caius.
> We all stand up against the spirit of Caesar,
> And in the spirit of men there is no blood.
> O that we then could come by Caesar's spirit
> And not dismember Caesar! But, alas,

Caesar must bleed for it. And, gentle friends,
Let's kill him boldly, but not wrathfully;
Let's carve him as a dish fit for the gods,
Not hew him as a carcass fit for hounds.

(II. 1. 166–74)

Brutus' self-delusion is in full stride, as he here defines his intentions in
terms which his honourable instinct can accept, and Shakespeare has
him continue, with monstrous illogic, to play a sort of Boniface to his
own Guido.

And let our hearts, as subtle masters do,
Stir up their servants to an act of rage
And after seem to chide 'em. This shall make
Our purpose necessary, and not envious;
Which so appearing to the common eyes,
We shall be call'd purgers, not murderers.

(II. 1. 175–80)

This curious idea, that our hearts are masters of our hands, but not
responsible for the deeds they do, is a clear evasion of responsibility,
but Brutus remains deluded, and Shakespeare concludes the scene by
displaying to the audience, as he had done with Casca at the end of
Act I, the encouragement which the world Brutus inhabits gives to his
faith in honour as a guide to behaviour. Shakespeare makes a very slight
change in Plutarch's account of the recruiting of Ligarius for the
conspiracy, but it is in its way one of the most revealing departures
from the source in the play. Plutarch reports Ligarius as saying:
'Brutus . . . if thou hast any great enterprise in hand worthy of thy-
self, I am whole' (IX. 254). There is nothing equivocal in this report,
for throughout Plutarch's account Brutus is the picture of republican
virtue. Shakespeare's Ligarius attests again to the pre-eminence in
Brutus' world of 'the name of honour'.

I am not sick, if Brutus have in hand
Any exploit worthy the name of honour.

(II. 1. 316–17)

Brutus' decision to kill Caesar and these three commands to the
conspirators display to the audience Brutus' implicit assumption that
his honour is a valid guide to action; the speeches of Brutus and of

65

Antony, after the murder, start developing the consequences of this assumption. In his speech to the mob, Brutus uses the word *honour* in two distinctly different, and familiar, ways. His argument, 'Not that I lov'd Caesar less, but that I lov'd Rome more', would, if sound, be sufficient. He states his love for Caesar and his fear of him briefly.

> As Caesar lov'd me, I weep for him; as he was fortunate, I rejoice at it; as he was valiant, I honour him; but – as he was ambitious, I slew him.
>
> (III. II. 24–6)

Honour, in this context, has an older and simpler meaning: external reward for and recognition of valour. It is the sort of honour the plebeians had rendered Caesar, and which the Tribunes had so distrusted, in scene i. But to justify his act, Brutus needs to demonstrate Caesar's ambition – or, more accurately, that whatever ambition he may have had was dangerous to the general good. To support his charge of ambition, however, Brutus only reminds the mob that he is an honourable man; if he is honourable, he implies, then his act must have been just.

> Romans, countrymen, and lovers, hear me for my cause, and be silent, that you may hear. Believe me for mine honour, and have respect to mine honour, that you may believe.
>
> (III. II. 13–16)

This is a familiar reversal, but this time it is Brutus' undoing. When agreeing to let Antony speak at Caesar's funeral, Brutus had assured Cassius:

> I will myself into the pulpit first
> And show the reason of our Caesar's death.
>
> (III. I. 236–7)

The 'reason' turns out to be that Brutus is an honourable man, and Antony attacks that reason ironically and successfully. His success, of course, depends on his appealing to the mob's self-interest, a success reported by Plutarch and demanded by historical fact. But the irony of his refrain:

> But Brutus says he was ambitious,
> And Brutus is an honourable man
>
> (III. II. 86–7)

is Shakespeare's addition. To instigate Antony's revenge, and to move the play forward to its resolution, Shakespeare has Antony choose to attack Brutus in the spot which the first half of the play has defined as the most vulnerable: his dependence on honour to justify his deed. The mob, to be sure, is fickle, but the fact that Antony is able to sway them does not necessarily suggest that the statements Shakespeare gives him are false. The play is clearly not concerned either to justify or to deny Antony's praise of Caesar. Caesar's devotion to his own image of himself is pompous; indeed Decius Brutus depends on and mocks that pomposity when, at II. 1. 202–11, he assures the conspirators that Caesar will be at the capitol. But Caesar's rigid commitment to his role is rather a parallel to Brutus' commitment to honour than an indication of tyranny. Certainly if Shakespeare had needed a tyrannous Caesar, he could have created one. Antony's funeral oration is less a definition of Caesar than a statement of Brutus' delusion.

> They that have done this deed are honourable.
> What private griefs they have, alas, I know not,
> That made them do it. They are wise and honourable,
> And will no doubt with reasons answer you.
>
> (III. II. 210–13)

When we next see Brutus, he has degenerated markedly, and the rest of the play is largely concerned to emphasize the tragic results of his obedience to the demands of honour. Cassius' statement is ironically just.

> Brutus, this sober form of yours hides wrongs. . . .
>
> (IV. II. 40)

The first wrong which Shakespeare displays has been variously interpreted, usually in an effort to demonstrate Brutus' nobility, but sometimes more sceptically. Brutus condemns Cassius for his method of getting money.

> Let me tell you, Cassius, you yourself
> Are much condemn'd to have an itching palm,
> To sell and mart your offices for gold
> To undeservers.
>
> (IV. III. 9–12)

Yet, some sixty lines later, Brutus condemns Cassius for not sending

67

him some of the money so evilly got. Brutus' behaviour here, which
has to some commentators seemed illogical, is consistent with his
behaviour throughout, and is indicative of the state to which his
singular adherence to honour has brought him.[5] Shakespeare has
developed this scene by making a typical modification of Plutarch's
account. In Plutarch, Brutus' request for money is met by Cassius,
against the advice of his advisers, and Plutarch does not connect a
quarrel with this request. The quarrel, in Plutarch, results only from
Brutus' condemnation and Cassius' support of Lucius Pella's 'robbery
and pilfery in his office'. Characteristically, Plutarch's Brutus is
determined to pursue the virtuous course.

> Brutus in contrary manner answered, that he [Cassius] should
> remember the Ides of March, at which time they slew Julius Caesar,
> who neither pilled nor polled the country, but only was a favorer
> and suborner of all them that did rob and spoil, by his countenance
> and authority. And if there were any occasion whereby they might
> honestly set aside justice and equity, they should have had more
> reason to have suffered Caesar's friends to have robbed and done
> what wrong and injury they had would than to bear with their own
> men. 'For then', said he, 'they could but have said we had been
> cowards, but now they may accuse us of injustice, beside the pains
> we take, and the danger we put ourselves into.' And thus may we
> see what Brutus' intent and purpose was.
>
> (IX. 288)

Shakespeare slightly but significantly modifies Plutarch to make his
Brutus, consistently assuming that virtue will follow, pursue the
honourable course.

> Remember March; the ides of March remember.
> Did not great Julius bleed for justice sake?
> What villain touched his body that did stab
> And not for justice? What, shall one of us,
> That struck the foremost man of all this world
> But for supporting robbers – shall we now
> Contaminate our fingers with base bribes,
> And sell the mighty space of our large honours
> For so much trash as may be grasped thus?
>
> (IV. III. 18–26)

The honourable course, though, is here made obviously faulty, for Brutus is after all demanding the same money which his honour had not permitted him to collect for himself.

> I did send to you
> For certain sums of gold, which you denied me;
> For I can raise no money by vile means.
>
> (IV. III. 69–71)

This is a familiar evasion of responsibility. The only difference between the Brutus here and the Brutus of the first and second acts is a difference in degree. We have seen how his concern for the name of honour misled him early in the play; Brutus' self-delusion is here becoming more evident and the effects of it more debilitating.

Brutus figures in five more episodes after this quarrel. The debate over tactics with Cassius (which provides the necessary narrative move to Philippi through another tactical mistake on Brutus' part) and the subsequent appearance of Caesar's ghost (who defines himself as Brutus' 'evil spirit' and warns that he will be seen again at Philippi), though brief, provide for and foreshadow the events of the final battle. The other three episodes in which Brutus figures, his reaction to the double revelation of Portia's death, the parley in the first scene of Act V, and, finally, his suicide, each display a Brutus whose sense of honour has become merely self-protective, isolated from any concern but its own preservation.

Whether Shakespeare intended the double revelation of Portia's death to stand will probably remain a source of debate,[6] but when seen in terms of the theme of honour, Brutus' separate reactions to the news are typical results of his determination to preserve the name of honour and as consistent with this character as the illogical demand for money from Cassius. Cassius first offers Brutus reproof.

> Of your philosophy you make no use
> If you give place to accidental evils.
>
> (IV. III. 145–6)

Brutus will have none of it.

> No man bears sorrow better. Portia is dead.
>
> (IV. III. 147)

Shakespeare may have intended this to be a self-righteous display of stoical fortitude, but the tone of the passage is ambiguous. The context is clear, though, and is important. Brutus and Cassius are alone on stage, and Brutus' remark, whether self-righteous or not, is a strictly private remark. Brutus' ruling concern with the name of honour is not touched, in this situation, by this remark – unless it be touched mildly, and privately, by Cassius' reproof. The next revelation of Portia's death is in a different context, and Brutus' concern for the name of honour is indeed touched. Brutus' second response is exactly the response which Messala expects of him, and it elicits appropriate praise from Messala. Brutus is here in a public situation, and he responds as his public 'image' demands he respond.

> *Bru.* Now as you are a Roman, tell me true.
> *Mes.* Then like a Roman bear the truth I tell;
> For certain she is dead, and by strange manner.
> *Bru.* Why, farewell, Portia. We must die, Messala.
> With meditating that she must die once,
> I have the patience to endure it now.
> *Mes.* Even so great men great losses should endure.
>
> (IV. III. 187–93)

The parley among Brutus, Cassius, Octavius, and Antony is brief but explicit. Shakespeare gives Antony, the first of the Caesarian party to speak, an angry and vengeful tone, but he also gives him statements which make it clear that the purpose of this parley is to display the motives of both sides – and statements which are in all important respects factual.

> In your bad strokes, Brutus, you give good words;
> Witness the hole you make in Caesar's heart,
> Crying 'Long live! Hail, Caesar!'
>
> (V. I. 30–2)

Octavius, less passionate, turns to the issue and announces the cause of his fighting.

> Come, come, the cause! If arguing make us sweat,
> The proof of it will turn to redder drops.
> Look,
> I draw a sword against conspirators.
> When think you that the sword goes up again?

Never, till Caesar's three-and-thirty wounds
Be well aveng'd, or till another Caesar
Have added slaughter to the sword of traitors.

(V. 1. 48–55)

The scene clearly demands a statement of Brutus' cause. Octavius'
'Come, come, the cause' and Antony's vengeful anger lead us to expect
a statement of purpose from Brutus. By disappointing that expectation
Shakespeare continues to develop the consequences of Brutus' commitment to honour. Missing are his concern for the general good and
his hatred of tyranny. Remaining is the same sort of concern for his
honourable name which Brutus has maintained since Cassius com-
plained that Caesar's name was 'sounded more' than Brutus'.

Bru. Caesar, thou canst not die by traitor's hands
    Unless thou bring'st them with thee.
Oct.   So I hope.
    I was not born to die on Brutus' sword.
Bru. O, if thou wert the noblest of thy strain,
    Young man, thou couldst not die more honourable.

(V. 1. 56–60)

Shakespeare has thus maintained the tragic irony of Brutus' delusion
throughout, and he makes the manner of Brutus' suicide the logical and
tragic conclusion of his career in the play. Cassius introduces the
question of suicide, asking Brutus if he intends to kill himself should
they lose the day. Brutus' paradoxical reply is typical. His first response
is based on one ideal, the Stoicism with which Shakespeare credited
him at the revelation of Portia's death and which Shakespeare there
put to much the same use. Brutus' devotion to this standard of behaviour seems compelling enough.

Even by the rule of that philosophy
By which I did blame Cato for the death
Which he did give himself – I know not how,
But I do find it cowardly and vile,
For fear of what might fall, so to prevent
The time of life – arming myself with patience
To stay the providence of some high powers
That govern us below.

(V. 1. 100–7)

Shakespeare, by having Cassius ask if Brutus will be content 'to be led in triumph/ Through the streets of Rome', puts Brutus' dilemma precisely. Brutus is now faced with the standard of behaviour which has considerably more hold over him than Stoicism does, so his reply is illogical only in the same way as his demand for money and his double response to Portia's death were illogical. Though he considers it 'cowardly and vile' to 'prevent the time of life', he will abandon that ideal rather than accept shame.

> No, Cassius, no. Think not, thou noble Roman,
> That ever Brutus will go bound to Rome.
> He bears too great a mind. (V. I. 110–12)

Brutus' devotion to honour has overcome him; he is so intent on preserving the name of honour that all other concerns are stripped from him. His irrational behaviour is most pitiable in his search for someone honourable enough to serve as the instrument of his suicide. Cassius has no such dilemma, a contrast which Shakespeare makes explicit.

> *Cas.* Come hither, sirrah.
> In Parthia did I take thee prisoner;
> And then I swore thee, saving of thy life,
> That whatsoever I did bid thee do,
> Thou shouldst attempt it. Come now, keep thine oath.
> Now be a freeman, and with this good sword,
> That ran through Caesar's bowels, search this bosom.
> (V. III. 36–42)

Shakespeare has Brutus ask three of his more exalted companions to hold the sword on which he means to kill himself, but has them each refuse him. So, typically announcing that he 'shall have glory by this losing day/ More than Octavius and Mark Antony/ By this vile conquest shall attain unto' (V. I. 36–8), Brutus is forced to turn to his servant Strato, who is not so exalted, but who will have to serve.

> I prithee, Strato, stay thou by thy lord.
> Thou art a fellow of a good respect;
> Thy life hath had some smatch of honour in it.
> Hold then my sword, and turn away thy face
> While I do run upon it. (V. v. 44–8)

Shakespeare thus makes Brutus' singular dependence on his sense of honour, which becomes self-protective and isolates Brutus from the reality of the world around him during the course of the play, the cause of his tragedy. Shakespeare also, of course, asserts Brutus' stature in every scene, providing a dual judgment of his protagonist which is necessary to the structure of the play. In a manner prophetic of the mature tragedies, the source of Brutus' nobility – his honour – is the source of his tragedy. Shakespeare places Brutus in a world compelled by the demands of honour, and he is at once the noblest citizen of that world and the most pitiable subject of its inverted ideals. After the decision to kill Caesar, each of these important scenes of the play dramatizes Brutus' moral and intellectual decay as being a direct consequence of his commitment to the name of honour, and each maintains the tragic irony of the play by surrounding Brutus with characters who all share some form of Casca's belief that honour, 'like richest alchemy', can change offence to virtue. Antony's final speech is but the last and most explicit instance both of the stature which Shakespeare has given Brutus and of the permissive context in which Brutus' tragic illusion operated.

> This was the noblest Roman of them all.
> All the conspirators save only he
> Did that they did in envy of great Caesar;
> He, only in a general honest thought
> And common good to all, made one of them.
> His life was gentle, and the elements
> So mix'd in him that Nature might stand up
> And say to all the world, 'This was a man!'
>
> (V. v. 68–75)

Notes to Chapter 3

[1] See above, pp. 26–9.

[2] Virgil K. Whitaker, *Shakespeare's Use of Learning* (San Marino, 1953), pp. 243 ff., argues that Shakespeare deliberately makes Brutus' first soliloquy irrational to provide for the false moral choice which Whitaker sees as the

heart of the tragedy. T. S. Dorsch, ed., *Julius Caesar* (Arden Shakespeare Series, London, 1955), p. xxxiii, also thinks that 'though [Brutus'] reasoning is false, his motives are of the loftiest. . . .' In a note to the speech, however, Dorsch records Dover Wilson's 'sensible elucidation of this soliloquy' (p. 33, n. to II.i.10–34), an elucidation which argues for the reasonableness of Brutus' conclusion.

[3] If it should be argued here that Shakespeare for some reason means this judgment actually to apply to Cicero – though it seems unlikely that he would be at pains to define a character who figures so little in the play – then it should be noted that such a Cicero would be but one more inhabitant of a world in which 'the name of honour' takes precedence over 'the general good'.

[4] Plutarch, *The Life of Marcus Brutus*, in *Plutarch's Lives*, tr. Sir Thomas North, ed. W. H. D. Rouse (London, 1899), IX.263–4. References in the text to Plutarch are to this edition.

[5] G. Ross Smith, 'Brutus, Virtue, and Will', *Shakespeare Quarterly*, X (1959), arguing that 'the central quality of Brutus is not his virtue [but] his will', explains the apparent illogicality as an instance of Brutus' 'self-righteous willfulness' (p. 377). Whitaker uses the same term to explain the same apparent illogicality. 'These lines suggest that Shakespeare took more pains to emphasize Brutus' self-righteous inconsistency than to construct a credible speech' (*Shakespeare's Use of Learning*, p. 236).

[6] Brents Stirling, '*Julius Caesar* in Revision', *Shakespeare Quarterly*, XIII (1962), argues that Shakespeare added one revelation when he revised the play, but sees no evidence that he intended to delete the existing account. 'Shakespeare', Stirling maintains, 'deliberately added both at the same time and made them contiguous' (p. 194). Warren D. Smith, 'The Duplicate Revelation of Portia's Death', *Shakespeare Quarterly*, IV (1953), pp. 153–61, provides a thorough summary of the critical debate, but his judgment that 'the dramatist intended [the duplicate revelation] to be unmistakable witness to the unselfishness, fortitude, and able generalship characteristic of Brutus in other parts of the play' is suspect.

Chapter 4

TROILUS and CRESSIDA
Mad Idolatry

In *Troilus and Cressida* Shakespeare initially presents his audience with Greeks and Trojans who have quite distinct problems. The Greeks, as everyone had known for centuries, can get on with winning the war only if they can persuade Achilles to fight. Shakespeare puts his absence in a peculiarly humanistic context by having Ulysses give voice to a series of moral commonplaces about 'degree', but the orthodox forms of virtue defined in Ulysses' speech, so useful to students of the history of ideas, virtually drop out of Greek discussions of the problem with that speech, and Achilles' grudging mind is changed, and changed again, and yet again for three quite different reasons. Shakespeare presents the audience with Trojans whose first council debates, likewise in humanistic terms, an issue also drawn from the legend; Hector, basing his argument on a set of assumptions drawn from the same fund of humanistic moral commonplaces that Shakespeare had Ulysses first introduce into the play, wants to give Helen back to Menelaus. That argument, too, marks the end of any pretence among the Trojans that orthodox morality has any effective control over men's behaviour. In both camps the unimpeachable standard of behaviour, to which all other motives for action are thereafter referred, is honour.

The pre-eminent role that honour plays in the lives of the characters on stage would no doubt have continued to seem normal or even inevitable to Shakespeare's first audiences, even – or particularly – if they were the sophisticated audiences at the Inns of Court. What would probably have startled them, and marked the play as unorthodox, is the sceptical, satirical attitude which the play develops towards the idea of honour. The basis of this scepticism and the object of much of the play's satire is the automatic and hopeless way the characters serve a code they have themselves created and which they know to have only the value they have subjectively assigned it. The play fully exploits a definition of honour thoroughly removed from the Aristotelian norm, a definition similar to that implied by Casca's observation that Brutus' 'countenance, like richest alchemy', will change offence to 'virtue and to worthiness'. It is, presumably, a definition of honour familiar enough to Shakespeare's audience to warrant this dramatic exploitation of it. Greville's *Inquisition upon Fame and Honour* includes this sort of honour in its survey of the various meanings the term had assumed, and argues for the practical usefulness of such a self-created ideal in this fallen world.[1] The most revealing sixteenth-century treatment of honour as a code independent of or, even, antithetical to the orthodox system of rational morality, however, is Tasso's *Jerusalem Delivered*. Tasso, it may be recalled, makes Godfrey, the commander of the crusading army, allegorically represent 'the Understanding', that is, the rational principle which controls the army, and makes Rinaldo, the chief soldier, allegorically represent Plato's 'Ireful Virtue', citing *The Republic*.

> The Ireful Virtue is that, which amongst all the powers of the mind, is less estranged from the nobility of the soul, insomuch that Plato, doubting, seeketh whether it differeth from reason or no.[2]

Tasso had his Plato confused in a way that instructs us about this aberrant meaning of the idea of honour as it developed in the Renaissance. Plato, to be sure, establishes passion, or the ireful virtue, as one of the three principles of the soul and describes it as 'wholly set on ruling and conquering and getting fame', but he concludes the argument by emphasizing the subordinate role this virtue plays.

> Both together will they not be the best defenders of the whole soul and the whole body against attacks from without; the one counselling, and the other fighting under his leader, and courageously executing his commands and counsels?[3]

Tasso, on the other hand, makes Rinaldo's honour independent of the ideals of political authority and reason, which Godfrey represents, and he brings these two to a confrontation which is never logically reconciled. In the fifth book of the poem, Rinaldo, commanded by honour, slays Gernando, who has insulted him. The demands of honour are clearly put in conflict with the demands of reason and order, for civil chaos is only narrowly averted. Friends of Gernando urge punishment.

> Arnoldo, minion of the Prince thus slain . . . saith,
> This Prince is murdered, for a quarrel vain,
> By young Rinaldo in his desperate wrath,
> And with that sword that should Christ's law maintain
> One of Christ's champions bold he killed hath,
>> And this he did in such a place and hour,
>> As if he scorned your [Godfrey's] rule, despised your power.
> And further adds, that he deserved death
> By law, and law should be inviolate . . .
> If he escape, that mischief would take breath,
> And flourish bold in spite of rule and state;
>> And that Gernando's friends would venge the wrong,
>> Although to justice that did first belong. . . .

(V. 33–4)

Godfrey determines to bring Rinaldo to trial. Rinaldo, immediately and wrathfully rejecting trial as dishonourable, arms to fight, but is persuaded to leave the camp to avert civil war. A reconciliation is not effected until Book XVIII, with Rinaldo's apology to Godfrey. But it is clear that this apology is not meant as a repudiation of the principles of honour. Should the same situation arise, Rinaldo would – indeed, must – take the same action, and his apology is illogically mixed with the assurance that what he did was necessary according to a standard of behaviour as valid as that of obedience to his king.

> Arrived where Godfrey to embrace him stood,
> 'My sovereign lord,' Rinaldo meekly said,
> 'To venge my wrongs against Gernando proud
> My honour's care provoked my wrath unstayed;
> But that I you displeased, my chieftain good,
> My thoughts yet grieve, my heart is still dismayed,
>> And here I come, prest all exploits to try
>> To make me gracious in your gracious eye.'

(XVIII. 1)

Tasso's extended allegorical treatment of honour as a standard of behaviour independent of reason does not attempt to resolve the dilemma involved; indeed, Tasso's appeal to Platonic authority to justify a definition of honour far removed from the orthodox view of it as the reward due to virtue suggests that he sees no dilemma. The effect of making Rinaldo the perfect man of this sort of honour is to give him a stature necessary to the plan of the poem and otherwise unavailable. In *Troilus and Cressida*, however, Shakespeare fully exploits the dilemma implicit in this aberrant and compelling code of behaviour. The Greeks, tutored by Ulysses and represented in the extremist form by Thersites, are made considerably more cynical in their response to the dilemmas and opportunities afforded by this sort of honour than the Trojans, who, urged on by Troilus and followed most pathetically by Hector, are made to obey like marionettes the demands of their self-imposed master. Shakespeare makes both obedient to the kind of honour Tasso had displayed in Rinaldo, a code, as Shakespeare develops it, independent of political authority, reason, and even, sometimes, common sense. Brutus had been left tragically unaware that the honourable instincts he obeyed were leading him into irrational behaviour. Dramatizing two quite distinct episodes from the Trojan legend, Shakespeare has his characters actively serve forms of love and honour which have the most pernicious effect on their behaviour.[4]

Aeneas brings the older, straightforward forms of love and honour into the play with his chivalric challenge to the Greek camp, though the hyperboles in which he announces the challenge provide a kind of self-parody.

> If there be one among the fair'st of Greece
> That holds his honour higher than his ease,
> That seeks his praise more than he fears his peril,
> That knows his valour and knows not his fear,
> That loves his mistress more than in confession
> With truant vows to her own lips he loves,
> And dare avow her beauty and her worth
> In other arms than hers – to him this challenge!
>
> (I. III. 265–72)

Ulysses, though, is made immediately to see that the challenge can be used to crop the 'seeded pride/ That hath to this maturity blown up/ In rank Achilles ...' (I. III. 316–18). Shakespeare has Ulysses deal with the matter as though honour, theoretically the prize due to victory, were too useful a commodity to be left to the exigencies of combat, however 'sportful'. Achilles is 'too insolent' to share the glory, should he win; the Greeks' honour would be tainted by the defeat of their best man, should he lose. Ulysses therefore determines that they, 'like merchants', should show their 'foulest wares,/ And think perchance they'll sell ...' (I. III, 359–60). The honour thus defined is clearly divorced from anything like virtue. It has taken on an importance independent of its origin, and as such it is so important that Ulysses is prepared to use the most devious means to obtain it, means which would be simply incompatible with such orthodox, Aristotelian principles of honour as are displayed, for instance, in Hotspur. Ulysses is never made to assume that the rational ideals of moral order which he articulated in his first speech will inevitably assert themselves in men's behaviour. He is made instead to assume that he can manipulate that behaviour by appealing to men's commitment to honour, as he does with Achilles and Ajax. His is a clever, pragmatic response to so subjective but compelling a code of behaviour, and Shakespeare juxtaposes it with the response he has Thersites bring into the play in the following scene. Thersites sees the arbitrary and shifting values that operate in his world as clearly as Ulysses does, but rather than Ulysses' pragmatic effort to give that world what shape he can, Thersites is made to remain cynical in practice as well as understanding. He chooses, in his first scene and throughout the play, to rail at rather than engage in this argument over a 'whore and a cuckold'.

The first scene in the Trojan camp explores in explicit detail the differences between honour so understood and orthodox ideas of rational morality. To Shakespeare's first audiences, accustomed at least in theory to justifying the important role honour plays in society by defining it as a consequence of virtuous action, the absolute antipathy between virtuous behaviour and honourable behaviour dramatized by this scene must have served to make the play more topical and contemporary than even Shakespeare's putting the moral statements of orthodox humanism into the mouths of Trojan and Greek heroes. Troilus displays almost exactly the sort of honour Tasso had Rinaldo figure forth in *Jerusalem Delivered*; the difference is that Shakespeare takes him to the logical conclusion of this position by having him explicitly argue that honour is a motive for behaviour superior to the dictates of reason.

> Nay, if we talk of reason,
> Let's shut our gates and sleep. Manhood and honour
> Should have hare hearts, would they but fat their thoughts
> With this cramm'd reason. Reason and respect
> Make livers pale and lustihood deject.
>
> (II. II. 46–50)

Faced with Hector's argument that Helen is not worth the cost, Troilus gives voice to the basic article in this subjective creed.

> What is aught but as 'tis valu'd?
>
> (II. II. 52)

Hector is ready with the orthodox argument. 'Value dwells not in particular will' (II. II. 53). The speech is as ringing a statement of humanistic ethics as Ulysses' had been earlier. It describes a moral universe, comprised of objective values which man's reason allows him to discover.

> 'Tis mad idolatry
> To make the service greater than the god;
> And the will dotes that is attributive
> To what infectiously itself affects
> Without some image of th' affected merit.
>
> (II. II. 53–60)

The scene is developed at length, and the distinction between Hector's orthodoxy, which assumes that man can act in accord with the universal values his reason discovers, and Troilus' honour, which assumes that value can be assigned to otherwise valueless objects by making them a matter of honour, is reiterated a sufficient number of times to prevent anyone in the audience from missing the point. Paris, for instance, discounting pleasure in Helen as his motive, 'would have the soil of her fair rape/Wip'd off in honourable keeping her' (II. II. 148–9). The debate is never logically resolved. Hector continues to know 'in way of truth' that the 'moral laws/ Of nature and of nations speak aloud/ To have her back return'd' (II. II. 184–6). He nevertheless determines 'to keep Helen still;/ For 'tis a cause that hath no mean dependence/ Upon our joint and several dignities' (II. II. 191–3). This is an illogical reversal, as has often been remarked, but just such illogical behaviour and its consequences are among the major objects of the play's satire.[5] The major characters in the 'war plot' act according to the demands of this strict master. Hector's reversal, rather than being unique, is the most telling blow. By making explicit Hector's understanding of the rational norms of virtuous behaviour, Shakespeare demonstrates the overwhelming appeal of the decadent norms of honourable behaviour.

Shakespeare has each of the major episodes of the war plot in the second half of the play – the dialogue in which Ulysses urges Achilles to fight, Hector's decision to fight in spite of Trojan protest, and Hector's death – display the consequences of obedience to this self-inflicted master. Because of his assumptions about honour, Achilles is ripe for Ulysses' scheme. Shakespeare makes those assumptions explicit.

> *Achil.* 'Tis certain, greatness, once fall'n out with fortune,
>   Must fall out with men too. What the declin'd is
>   He shall as soon read in the eyes of others
>   As feel in his own fall; for men, like butterflies,
>   Show not their mealy wings but to the summer;
>   And not a man, for being simply man
>   Hath any honour, but honour for those honours
>   That are without him, as place, riches, and favour,
>   Prizes of accident as oft as merit;
>   Which when they fall, as being slippery standers,
>   The love that lean'd on them as slippery too,
>   Do one pluck down another, and together
>   Die in the fall.
>
> (III. iii. 75–87)

Shakespeare has thus provided Achilles with the same understanding of honour which Troilus had expressed by having him assume that honour springs from transitory and accidental causes rather than permanent and necessary ones. Ulysses' task, which is to prompt Achilles to action by persuading him that his honour is at the stake, is accommodated by this view of honour. Shakespeare develops the scene by having Ulysses move from a strightforward, Platonic definition of honour to the definition he requires to persuade Achilles to act.

>   A strange fellow here
>   Writes me, that man – how dearly ever parted,
>   How much in having, or without or in –
>   Cannot make boast to have that which he hath,

Nor feels not what he owes, but by reflection;
As when his virtues, aiming upon others,
Heat them, and they retort that again
To the first giver.

(III. III. 95–102)[6]

This Platonic idea is a simple and familiar one; man does not know his virtue but by its reflection. Ulysses, much as Cassius had done with Brutus during their first dialogue, changes *reflection* to *applause* and thereby begins the shift in emphasis which is the scene's concern.

I do not strain at the position,
It is familiar, but at the author's drift,
Who, in his circumstance, expressly proves
That no man is the lord of anything,
Though in and of him there be much consisting,
Till he communicate his parts to others;
Nor doth he of himself know them for aught
Till he behold them formed in the applause
Where th' are extended. . . .

(III. III. 112–20)

The implications of this shift are made immediately apparent, for Ulysses applauds Ajax, whom the play clearly judges a braggart and buffoon, and implies that that applause and the applause he will gain by fighting Hector will provide Ajax with greater honour than Achilles. Achilles sees the danger.

I do believe it; for they [the Greek generals] pass'd by me
As misers do by beggars; neither gave to me
Good word nor look. What, are my deeds forgot?

(III. III. 142–44)

Ulysses, who knows his man, has appealed only to Achilles' desire for honour, leaving conspicuously absent any appeal for Achilles to fight for the common good of the Greek cause. He now sets out to prove that honour is always to be sought, for it is always at the stake.

Time hath, my lord, a wallet at his back,
Wherein he puts alms for oblivion,
A great-siz'd monster of ingratitudes.

Those scraps are good deeds past, which are devour'd
As fast as they are made, forgot as soon
As done. Perseverance, dear my lord,
Keeps honour bright. To have done is to hang
Quite out of fashion, like a rusty mail
In monumental mock'ry. Take the instant way;
For honour travels in a strait so narrow,
Where one but goes abreast. Keep then the path,
For emulation hath a thousand sons
That one by one pursue. If you give way,
Or hedge aside from the direct forthright,
Like to an ent'red tide, they all rush by
And leave you hindmost. . . .
                              Let not virtue seek
Remuneration for the thing it was!
For beauty, wit,
High birth, vigour of bone, desert in service,
Love, friendship, charity, are subjects all
To envious and calumniating Time.

(III. III. 145–74)

The virtues described here are merely transitory occasions on which one can acquire honour, and Achilles never doubts that it is honour, not virtue, that is to be sought. He has, however, another factor to consider. His love for Polyxena, Priam's daughter, forbids his going to war. Ulysses easily overcomes Achilles' reluctance by pointing out that honour has a higher claim on Achilles' actions than love has. Shakespeare continues to keep any mention of the good Achilles might do the Greek cause out of Ulysses' argument; the emphasis is on the reputation to be gained from action.

And better would it fit Achilles much
To throw down Hector than Polyxena.
But it must grieve young Pyrrhus now at home
When fame shall in our islands sound her trump
And all the Greekish girls shall tripping sing
'Great Hector's sister did Achilles win,
But our great Ajax bravely beat down him.'

(III. III. 207–13)

83

Achilles, though he has yet to make his choice, sees the danger in exactly the terms that Ulysses proposes.

> *Achil.* Shall Ajax fight with Hector?
> *Patr.* Ay, and perhaps receive much honour by him.
> *Achil.* I see my reputation is at stake;
>   My fame is shrewdly gor'd.
>
> (III. III. 225–8)

The pursuit of honour as it is here defined, Achilles' vow to Polyxena, and his anger at Patroclus' death are all conspicuously irrelevant to the general Greek cause, just as Troilus' appeal to the Trojans to preserve their honour is antithetical both to their common welfare and to the dictates of reason. Shakespeare, throughout the play, has kept the virtuous course apparent; the war is an unjust one, and Helen should be returned. The Trojan council has made this clear from the rational point of view, and various minor characters have made it clear that from the Greek point of view Helen is not worth the blood she costs. 'All the argument', Thersites announces, 'is a whore and a cuckold' (II. III. 66). Less suspect, Diomedes responds to Paris' question, 'Who . . . merits fair Helen best,/ Myself or Menelaus?' (IV. I. 53–4), with a bitter denunciation of Helen's worth and of the war fought over her.

> *Dio.*   Both alike.
> He merits well to have her that doth seek her,
> Not making any scruple of her soilure,
> With such a hell of pain and world of charge;
> And you as well to keep her, that defend her,
> Not palating the taste of her dishonour,
> With such a costly loss of wealth and friends.
> He, like a puling cuckold, would drink up
> The lees and dregs of a flat tamed piece;
> You, like a lecher, out of whorish loins
> Are pleas'd to breed out your inheritors.
> Both merits pois'd, each weighs nor less nor more;
> But he as he, the heavier for a whore.
> *Par.* You are too bitter to your country-woman.
> *Dio.* She's bitter to her country. Hear me, Paris:
> For every false drop in her bawdy veins

A Grecian's life hath sunk; for every scruple
Of her contaminated carrion weight
A Troyan hath been slain. Since she could speak,
She hath not given so many good words breath
As for her Greeks and Troyans suff'red death.

(IV. I. 54–74)

Whatever just motives the Greeks originally may have had are outside
the context of the play; within the play, their motives are all based on
'honour'. The Trojan council explicitly overthrows the 'moral laws/
Of nature and of nations' in order to serve the contrary demands of
honour. In this context, the terrible thing is that the standard of
behaviour which the characters have created for themselves has become
their master, and they adhere to it with the efficiency of robots. Thus,
not only has the war outgrown its cause, but also the demand for
honour has outgrown the war. Ulysses does not make the mistake of
appealing to Achilles to help end the war; he appeals to Achilles'
demand for honour. Hector, most pathetically, obeys honour's
command even though clear warning is given him that doing so means
Troy's defeat. Shakespeare explicitly makes honour, rather than
Trojan victory, Hector's purpose.

> *Hect.* Be gone, I say. The gods have heard me swear.
> *Cas.* The gods are deaf to hot and peevish vows. . . .
> *And.* O, be persuaded! Do not count it holy
> To hurt by being just. It is lawful,
> For we would give much, to use violent thefts
> And rob in the behalf of charity.
> *Cas.* It is the purpose that makes strong the vow;
> But vows to every purpose must not hold.
> Unarm, sweet Hector.
> *Hect.*　　　　Hold you still, I say.
> Mine honour keeps the weather of my fate.
> Life every man holds dear, but the dear man
> Holds honour far more precious-dear than life.

(V. III. 15–28)

When the antagonists finally meet, Shakespeare contrasts their
behaviour so as to summarize the tone the play has been developing.
Achilles' behaviour, though brutal, is characteristic. His commitment

85

to honour, under Ulysses' tutelage, is commitment to a commodity which it is necessary to have; the means by which one obtains that commodity are no concern of his. Killing Hector buys honour for him.

> Strike, fellows, strike! This is the man I seek.
> [Hector *falls*.]
> So, Ilion, fall thou next! Now, Troy, sink down!
> Here lies thy heart, thy sinews, and thy bone.
> On, Myrmidons, and cry you all amain,
> 'Achilles hath the mighty Hector slain.'

(V. VIII. 10–14)

Given his understanding of honour, there is no other conceivable way for him to behave. Hector, on the other hand, a moment or two earlier has given Achilles opportunity to pause, and we already know from Troilus that Hector has a 'vice of mercy'. His commitment to honour, though as thorough, is less cynical than Achilles'. He deludes himself the more thoroughly, and is destroyed. His destruction, of course, is demanded by the legend, but Shakespeare justifies it by making Hector a part – indeed, the most pathetic part, for he is earlier given the wisdom to know better – of this frustrating world in which men create their own standards of value only to become slaves to that creation.

Notes to Chapter 4

[1] See above, pp. 29–31.

[2] Torquato Tasso, *Jerusalem Delivered*, tr. Edward Fairfax (1600), Henry Morley (London, 1890), p. 441. Quotations in the text are from this edition.

[3] Plato, *The Republic*, IX.581, IV.442. *The Dialogues of Plato*, tr. B. Jowett (3rd edition, New York, 1937); tr. B. Jowett (London, 1970).

[4] Paul N. Siegel, *Shakespeare in His Time and Ours*, pp. 138–44, thinks the Trojans, after Hector's rational argument fails, act according to the 'neo-chivalric cult of honor'. Although he earlier argues that *Troilus and Cressida* is one of five plays in which Shakespeare treats this 'current concept of honor as a false cult' (p. 122), he also believes that when Troy and the sort of honour it represents fall to Achilles, 'the utter barbarian without a sense of

honor at all' (p. 144), 'with Troy goes something fine and grand' (p. 139). Siegel also thinks that Troilus' idea of honour, which 'sets reason aside', is identical with Hotspur's, which character he also places in the neo-chivalric ranks.

[5] Jean Gagen, in 'Hector's Honor', *Shakespeare Quarterly*, XIX (1968), pp. 129–37, cites several of the critics who have found Hector's reversal irrational, but, citing as evidence various Renaissance justifications of the duel, she argues that Hector's reversal is similarly justified. Gagen, another dichotomist, argues that 'the Renaissance humanist thought of honor in a two-fold sense: honor had an outward form and an inner essence. The inner essence of honor was virtue or justice – justice being a comprehensive term covering all the moral virtues' (p. 131). Honour, the argument continues, became so attached to valour that it was valued at the expense of the other virtues; the duel reflects the two-fold view of honour, for if the reward justly merited by a man were not forthcoming, or for some other reason his reputation were endangered, he must protect his honour. Professor Gagen then cites evidence that 'many Renaissance humanists sanctioned the breaking of the laws of the land as well as the Christian moral code to avenge insults to a gentleman's honor' (p. 133), and concludes that Hector's reversal is justified for the same reason. 'Those critics [who think *Troilus and Cressida* bitter and disillusioned] would perhaps be forced to modify their views if they considered the close relationship between Hector's discussion of honor and Renaissance discussions of the ethics of the duel. They might then see Hector's dilemma as one which many Renaissance gentlemen had confronted and his decision one which Renaissance humanists themselves had often made without any sense of having shamefully abandoned their ideals' (p. 137). There is no doubt that a variety of Renaissance spokesmen for honour justified duelling, even in a bad cause, to protect one's reputation. There is, on the other hand, no evidence at all that Shakespeare intended to suggest that Hector's reputation is somehow at stake. 'No man lesser fears the Greeks than I' (II.ii.8), Hector remarks, and his agreeing that keeping Helen is 'a cause that hath no mean dependence/Upon our joint and several dignities' is unexpected and illogical largely because Hector's reputation and valour have nowhere been questioned. Shakespeare has Troilus accuse Helenus of cowardice in a speech which could not conceivably have been directed at Hector, whose reputation for valour and whose heroic stature remain unblemished by the scene. Hector's reason for following the course he knows to be irrational and unjust is not that, as Gagen's argument asserts, 'the imputation of cowardice is a wrong too grievous for mortal man to bear' (p. 137). No such imputation has been made. The play deals very sceptically with such standards of behaviour as Professor Gagen cites from the duelling treatises; the sort of behaviour which Hector's sudden and illogical obedience to honour represents is among the origins of that scepticism.

⁶ Attempts to identify the 'strange fellow' have produced no unanimity of opinion. Hardin Craig, in a note to the line in *The Complete Works of Shakespeare* (Scott, Foresman, 1957), p. 883, remarks that Churton Collins had identified the 'fellow' as Plato, but T. W. Baldwin, in an appendix to the New Variorum Edition, eds. Harold N. Hillebrand and T. W. Baldwin (Philadelphia and London, 1953), traces the history of the dispute and disagrees with Collins' identification. Baldwin argues that the idea expressed by Ulysses was a literary commonplace of the day. 'It is surely plain', Baldwin further remarks, 'that the proposition of Achilles is not that of Ulysses, and that Shakespeare presents the former as missing the idea of the latter while professing to assent to it' (p. 412).

Chapter 5

HAMLET
The Motives of Tragedy

Hamlet's dilemma initially is that the values which his world accepts and which it expects him to accept have no apparent effect on the behaviour he sees around him. Shakespeare, by facing Hamlet with the call to action which the Ghost's demand for revenge initiates, sets him on a play-long inquiry into the values of his world in his effort to discover a valid basis on which action of any kind may be undertaken. Shakespeare puts three other characters, Fortinbras, Laertes, and Ophelia, in circumstances closely resembling Hamlet's. Similar de- mands are made on them to accept conventional modes of behaviour, and each loses his father through violent and unnatural means. Shakespeare thus allows himself to dramatize three separate responses to a dilemma which calls for action, and, thereby, to dramatize the consequences of responses which he has Hamlet contemplate, but reject. We know little of Fortinbras' motives until late in the play, but the early reports of his actions show us a character who makes a familiar response to the demands of honour. He, like Troilus, seeks honour on the battlefield regardless of the cause of the war. Horatio first reports that Fortinbras intends to go to war to recover the lands lost by King Hamlet's victory over King Fortinbras. As Voltimand later reports, Fortinbras is easily stripped of that intention, but the plans for war remain intact. Revenging his father's death is never made part of his motive; he is, indeed, provided with no motive beyond the mere pursuit of honour.

> Upon our first, he [Norway] sent out to suppress
> His nephew's levies; which to him appear'd
> To be a preparation 'gainst the Polack;
> But, better look'd into, he truly found

It was against your Highness [Claudius]: whereat griev'd,
... sends out arrests
On Fortinbras; which he, in brief, obeys. ...
Whereon old Norway, overcome with joy,
Gives him threescore thousand crowns in annual fee
And his commission to employ those soldiers,
So levied as before, against the Polack. ...

(II. ii. 61–75)

Late in Act IV, Hamlet explicitly contemplates Fortinbras' action as a possible solution to his own dilemma. Fortinbras' example suggests to Hamlet that he might assign value subjectively, a clear solution to his failure to discover objective validity in the values of his world. But Hamlet's final solution is not 'to find quarrel in a straw/ When honour's at the stake'. If it were, *Hamlet*, like *Troilus and Cressida*, would remain satirical and cynical, rather than tragic.[1]

Theodore Spencer has argued persuasively that Hamlet's dilemma can best be understood in terms of the widespread Renaissance understanding of the contrast between appearance and reality.

> In Hamlet [the orthodox beliefs] are not in the background, they are an essential part of the hero's consciousness, and his discovery that they are not true, his awareness of the conflict between what theory taught and what experience proves, wrecks him.[2]

Though rewarding and informative, this argument suggests a gradual discovery on Hamlet's part which is simply not present in the play. Hamlet does not learn through experience that real evil exists under the appearance of good; he assumes this from the beginning.

O God! God!
How weary, stale, flat, and unprofitable
Seem to me all the uses of this world!
Fie on't! ah, fie! 'tis an unweeded garden
That grows to seed; things rank and gross in nature
Possess it merely.

(I. ii. 132–7)

This assumption is a part of the melancholy which Shakespeare is at pains to assign Hamlet from the outset. His experience is a tragic one;

to see Hamlet, as Spencer's argument forces him to do, as a man shattered by the recognition that things are not as they seem is to make the play pathetic, not tragic. Furthermore, a great many things are precisely as they seem. Claudius, though condemned as a murderer, expects and receives, from all but Hamlet, the service due to him as a king. Ophelia, though Hamlet thinks her guilty of the same frailty of which he accuses his mother, is the picture of a dutiful daughter in her obedient response to her father's command. Rosencrantz and Guildenstern, though Hamlet thinks their alliance with Claudius a betrayal, think Hamlet mad and, obeying the King's command, are trying to deliver him from that madness. This mixture of good and evil and this display of orthodox virtues – such as obedience – which prove harmful are too complex for the labels *appearance* and *reality* to disjoin. It is just this complexity, from the point of view of the Prince, that makes Fortinbras' example an appealing one. Desperate to find a valid basis for action, and unable to discover where objective validity rests, Hamlet sees in honour a subjective basis for action which would allow him to ignore the inscrutable values of his world. One of the measures of Hamlet's tragic stature is that this expedient will not serve.

The appeal of this expedient is shown in unadulterated form in Fortinbras. Shakespeare gives Hamlet a soliloquy in which to contemplate the sort of honour Fortinbras represents as a solution to his dilemma. Shakespeare will have Hamlet in the graveyard scene explicitly reject this sort of honour as a motive for action; here he undercuts the idea by making Fortinbras' sort of honour clearly incompatible with the 'godlike reason' which Hamlet first considers in the soliloquy.

> What is a man,
> If his chief good and market of his time
> Be but to sleep and feed? A beast, no more.
> Sure he that made us with such large discourse,
> Looking before and after, gave us not
> That capability and godlike reason
> To fust in us unus'd.
>
> (IV. IV. 33–9)

This is a general and orthodox inquiry into the bases of men's actions. Hamlet next turns to the motives he in particular has for action, and wonders that he has as yet failed to act, since he has 'cause, and will,

91

and strength, and means,/ To do't'. Hamlet is frankly puzzled over his failure to act, and the reason he is puzzled is that he has as yet found no unimpeachably valid principle which can justify action of any kind. Fortinbras represents an escape from this dilemma, for he acts by assigning a value, honour, to an otherwise valueless cause. It is consequently in something like desperation that Hamlet considers the honour that Fortinbras accepts as his sole motive. But Fortinbras' 'divine ambition', his indifference to the outcome of his war, and his willingness to expose himself – and twenty thousand men – to death for nothing, 'for an eggshell', are clearly motives incompatible with 'godlike reason'. The service, for Fortinbras, has become greater than the god. Honour is nevertheless an appealing and accessible principle, for it permits its adherents to act when rational men would be stymied by their inability to find any justification for action.

> Rightly to be great
> Is not to stir without great argument,
> But greatly to find quarrel in a straw
> When honour's at the stake.

(IV. IV. 53–6)

Although Hamlet knows he has reasons more compelling than Fortinbras', it is not for those reasons nor for the sake of honour that he is finally made to act. Nor does Fortinbras provide the only sort of honour which the play has Hamlet contemplate and reject. Other aspects of honour, familiar to the audience, are major parts of the responses of the other two young people whom Shakespeare has put in situations parallel with Hamlet's.

Laertes' reaction to his father's death is precisely what the Ghost – and the dramatic tradition of revenge tragedies – had demanded of Hamlet. Laertes knows that honour demands that he revenge his father, and he is prepared to go to any lengths to execute that revenge. This revenge, like Ophelia's obedience, is one of the commonplaces of the ethics of honour which Shakespeare treats so sceptically in the play by having Hamlet question values in which the other characters – and orthodox moral speculation – have implicit faith. Laertes' first anger springs from his assumption, similar to one that Lear will make, that there exists a 'natural' relationship between parent and child which requires his honourable anger.

That drop of blood that's calm proclaims me bastard;
Cries cuckold to my father; brands the harlot
Even here between the chaste unsmirched brows
Of my true mother.

(IV. v. 115–18)

Claudius counters by relying on another 'natural' relationship, but one which is here contradictory; he defines the relationship between himself as king and Laertes as subject.

Let him go, Gertrude. Do not fear our person.
There's such divinity doth hedge a king
That treason can but peep to what it would,
Acts little of his will.

(IV. v. 120–3)

Laertes understands, but he chooses to act in his role as son rather than in his role as subject.

I'll not be juggled with:
To hell, allegiance! vows, to the blackest devil!
Conscience and grace, to the profoundest pit!
I dare damnation. To this point I stand,
That both the worlds I give to negligence,
Let come what comes; only I'll be reveng'd
Most thoroughly for my father.

(IV. v. 128–34)

Laertes is thus able to make a choice which Hamlet was unwilling to make – or unable to make; the point is moot here. He chooses to pursue his revenge on the grounds that the natural relationship between son and father demands that the son revenge his father's unnatural death. Laertes' single-mindedness, like Fortinbras' willingness to dare all for honour's sake, is from a certain point of view appealing in comparison with Hamlet's apparent unwillingness to act when faced with the problem of revenge. But it provides no answer to Hamlet's complex questions, and, as the play judges it, serves to destroy its possessor. Laertes, because of his single-minded commitment to honourable revenge, can be manipulated by Claudius in familiar fashion. Never questioning the justice of his cause and the validity of his honourable motives, Laertes is easily persuaded to adopt the underhanded and dishonourable means Claudius proposes. Claudius does offer Laertes generous conditions.

G

93

Go but apart,
Make choice of whom your wisest friends you will,
And they shall hear and judge 'twixt you and me.
If by direct or by collateral hand
They find us touch'd, we will our kingdom give,
Our crown, our life, and all that we call ours,
To you in satisfaction. . . .

(IV. v. 198–204)

In a parallel scene early in the play, Claudius had made precisely this kind of appeal to Hamlet when trying to persuade him to stop mourning his father. Claudius there, too, argues that Hamlet has but one reasonable way to act.

But to persever
In obstinate condolement is a course
Of impious stubbornness. 'Tis unmanly grief;
It shows a will most incorrect to heaven,
A heart unfortified, a mind impatient,
An understanding simple and unschool'd. . . .

(I. II. 92–7)

And he offers the same sort of practical reward to Hamlet should he take the reasonable course.

We pray you throw to earth
This unprevailing woe, and think of us
As of a father; for let the world take note,
You are the most immediate to our throne. . . .

(I. II. 106–9)

Shakespeare has Hamlet, however, largely ignore Claudius' argument; Hamlet's decision to remain in Elsinore is in response to Gertrude's request, not to the King's. Laertes, late in the play faced with precisely the same kind of argument, succumbs, and from that moment Shakespeare displays him as a sort of marionette, moving as the demands of honour direct. He had begun this scene in angry determination to exact the revenge that honour requires; he leaves it bathetically, seemingly concerned only that the forms of honour due to his father had not been paid.

94

His means of death, his obscure funeral –
No trophy, sword, nor hatchment o'er his bones,
No noble rite nor formal ostentation, –
Cry to be heard, as 'twere from heaven to earth,
That I must call't in question.

(IV. v. 208–12)

Immediately before the duel scene, Shakespeare again brings on stage a Laertes whose freedom of choice has been denied by his commitment to honour; he must submit his case, in what the audience would no doubt have recognized as a familiar part of the code, to some 'masters, of known honour'.[3]

> I am satisfied in nature,
> Whose motive in this case should stir me most
> To my revenge. But in terms of honour
> I stand aloof, and will no reconcilement,
> Till by some elder masters, of known honour,
> I have a voice and precedent of peace,
> To keep my name ungor'd.

(V. II. 230–6)

This announcement is made, it should be recalled, by a Laertes whose honourable commitment to revenge his father's death has led him into the most dishonourable of schemes, an irony compounded by his belated awareness that the honour which he so dutifully serves might have misled him.

Laer. My lord, I'll hit [Hamlet] now.
King.　　　　I do not think't.
Laer. [*aside*] And yet it is almost against my conscience.

(V. II. 281–2)

Dying, Laertes says 'the King, the King's to blame', but he must accept a considerable portion of the guilt himself. His unqualified commitment to revenge, understood as honourable and just, is precisely what the Ghost demands and Hamlet, in his soliloquy after the Ghost exits, promises. But in Laertes, Shakespeare dramatizes the nature and consequences of this commitment, and judges it pernicious.

By making Ophelia Polonius' daughter and therefore conventionally subject to his authority, rather than retaining the paid courtesan of the source, Shakespeare creates another character who displays the nature and consequences of a course of action, widely and conventionally approved, which is available to Hamlet. Shakespeare introduces the question of Ophelia's obedience to her father in terms that have no apparent relevance to anything else in the play. If she does not obey, she will succumb to Hamlet's supposed advances at the expense of her chastity. This attitude towards the honour of women was a conventional part of speculation about the idea; by introducing it, Shakespeare makes all three of Hamlet's young counterparts, Ophelia, Laertes, and Fortinbras, respond to demands remarkably similar to those made on Hamlet by having them choose what was pervasively thought of as the honourable course. As we have seen,[4] Renaissance speculation on the matter considered the only virtue of which a woman could be capable, and therefore the only source of her honour, to be the protection of her chastity. Introducing Ophelia, Shakespeare develops extensively this commonplace identification of honour and female chastity. Like all the other commonplace values he introduces into the play, he puts this one severely to the test.

Shakespeare first defines the connection between honour and chastity through Laertes' eyes. Laertes does not distrust Hamlet's motives, but he thinks Hamlet's will not his own; he therefore advises Ophelia to be aware of the circumstances in which Hamlet finds himself.

> Then if he says he loves you,
> It fits your wisdom so far to believe it
> As he in his particular act and place
> May give his saying deed; which is no further
> Than the main voice of Denmark goes withal.
> Then weigh what loss your honour may sustain
> If with too credent ear you list his songs,
> Or lose your heart, or your chaste treasure open
> To his unmast'red importunity.

(I. III. 24–32)

This definition is a complex one, for it is as illustrative of Laertes as it is of Ophelia. Laertes makes precisely the same kind of assumption here as he makes later on by appealing to 'some elder masters, of known honour'. He assumes that man's commitment to a set of maxims and precepts, among them honour, is a safer guide than reason. Indeed, he

further asserts; women cannot escape dishonour if their virtue depend
on their own defences.

> Fear it, Ophelia, fear it, my dear sister,
> And keep you in the rear of your affection,
> Out of the shot and danger of desire.
> The chariest maid is prodigal enough
> If she unmask her beauty to the moon.
> Virtue itself scapes not calumnious strokes.
> The canker galls the infants of the spring,
> Too oft before their buttons be disclos'd. . . .
> Be wary then; best safety lies in fear.

(I. III. 33-43)

The play is here not so concerned with sexual morality as it is with the
orthodox demand that Ophelia obey proper male authority. That
Ophelia is controlled by her commitment to these ideas – that her
chastity is her honour, that she must preserve her honour at all costs,
and that she is incapable of preserving her honour unaided – is made
abundantly clear when Polonius takes up the theme that Laertes had
introduced. Before turning Polonius' attention to Ophelia's honour,
Shakespeare demonstrates that the old man is sententious for precisely
the same reason that Laertes is misguided and self-destructive; the
precepts to which he unflaggingly gives voice are for him as un-
questionable as the demands of honour will later be for Laertes.
Polonius, of course, is a comic extreme of this debility, but it is the
same kind of debility, and Ophelia is an easy victim. Hamlet, she
reports, has 'importun'd [her] with love/ In honourable fashion'
(I. III. 110-11). Shakespeare has chosen, however, to have Ophelia
report rather than to dramatize Hamlet's 'tenders of affection'. The
issue, consequently, is not whether they were 'sterling', for the scene
is not concerned to define Hamlet's love for Ophelia, but rather to
display the obedience which Polonius demands and Ophelia proffers.
Obedience to her father, in the effort to retain the honour her chastity
provides her, is the clear duty of the Renaissance gentlewoman, and
Ophelia is from that point of view choosing the most appropriate and
virtuous course. The scene, of course, immediately undercuts this
choice by making clear the difference between Ophelia's substantive
argument that Hamlet's 'tenders of affection' were honestly meant and
Polonius' reliance on a sort of conventional suspicion, which he even

manages to turn into a maxim, thereby establishing familiar moral ground for himself.

> I do know,
> When the blood burns, how prodigal the soul
> Lends the tongue vows. These blazes, daughter,
> Giving more light than heat, extinct in both
> Even in their promise, as it is a-making,
> You must not take for fire. From this time
> Be something scanter of your maiden presence. . . .
> I would not, in plain terms, from this time forth,
> Have you so slander any moment leisure
> As to give words or talk with the Lord Hamlet.
>
> (I. III. 115–34)

Ophelia obeys. Her obedience is both a conventional recognition of parental authority and an equally conventional acquiescence in the belief that, to remain virtuous, she must be kept from making any choice, for she should certainly make the wrong one. This is clearly virtue by rote, not by reason, and Shakespeare has it draw Ophelia into serious trouble. Loving Hamlet, she becomes, however unwittingly, an agent in the hands of Claudius and Polonius. Much of the nunnery scene focuses, whether Hamlet's anger at Ophelia be illogical or not,[5] on the deception which underlies and destroys honesty, a dilemma which Hamlet in the midst of his quest for some valid principle of behaviour in his enigmatic world views with particular bitterness.

> Ay, truly; for the power of beauty will sooner transform honesty from what it is to a bawd than the force of honesty can translate beauty into his likeness. This was sometime a paradox, but now the time gives it proof. I did love you once.
>
> (III. I. 111–15)

'We are oft to blame in this', Shakespeare has Polonius, quite out of character, remark to Ophelia before Hamlet's entrance, 'that with devotion's visage/ And pious action we do sugar o'er/ The devil himself' (III. I. 46–9). And Claudius, made for the first time to express his guilt to the audience, contributes to the scene's central concern with the effect of deception on honesty.

[Aside]   O, 'tis too true!
How smart a lash that speech doth give my conscience!
The harlot's cheek, beautied with plast'ring art,
Is not more ugly to the thing that helps it
Than is my deed to my most painted word.
O heavy burden!

(III. i. 49–54)

The scene is aptly summarized by Hamlet's cynical view of a world in which chastity, however pure, cannot 'escape calumny', and his anger at the dishonest posturings which have created that world.

I have heard of your paintings too, well enough. God hath given you one face, and you make yourselves another. You jig, you amble, and you lisp; you nickname God's creatures and make your wantonness your ignorance. Go to, I'll no more on't! it hath made me mad.

(III. i. 142–6)

Ophelia's guilt is not maliciously intended – or, even, conscious. Neither, however, is Laertes'. She, like him, has been led on by her willingness to pursue what the play defines and what was widely considered the honourable course. In her case, her death is as neatly symbolic as Laertes' underhanded and despicable plot to recover his family's honour. When her father, to whom she had handed over her faculties of choice, is killed, she loses her wits and can take no action at all, even to save her life. It is tempting to think that Shakespeare had this connection in mind when he wrote Laertes' response to Ophelia's madness.

O heavens! is't possible, a young maid's wits
Should be as mortal as an old man's life?

(IV. v. 157–8)

By means of these three separate responses to a dilemma similar to Hamlet's, Shakespeare has provided himself with an effective frame for the complex response he gives to Hamlet. *Hamlet* dramatizes the Prince's attempt to gain an understanding of his world sufficient to provide him with a valid basis for action. Shakespeare makes clear the universal difficulty of this attempt by showing us three characters who make more conventional responses. Ophelia finds a basis for action in obedience to parental authority and to a series of precepts which she unhesitatingly and conventionally accepts; this abdication of individual responsibility destroys her and contributes to the inscrutable and

99

destructive world which confronts Hamlet. Laertes finds a basis for action in what he uncritically assumes to be his 'natural' duty to revenge his father; this assumption destroys his freedom of choice by making him a slave to the demands of honour, and he is unwittingly led to his own destruction. Fortinbras is not concerned with discovering a valid basis for action; he assigns value – honour conceived as an end in itself – to whatever straw is available and proceeds to act on the basis of that honour. Unlike the other two, Fortinbras, apparently, succeeds. It is consequently necessary to examine more closely the nature of Hamlet's dilemma and of Fortinbras' apparent success to understand why Fortinbras' example will not serve.

Hamlet's first soliloquy is relatively straightforward. He longs for annihilation.

> O that this too too solid flesh would melt,
> Thaw, and resolve itself into a dew!
> Or that the Everlasting had not fix'd
> His canon 'gainst self-slaughter!
>
> (I. II. 129–32)

He explains his longing by describing the particular things, 'rank and gross in nature', which possess this world: his mother's marriage was over-hasty, but it was also incredible, for Claudius is clearly inferior to her first husband. Hamlet is incredulous, for he sees that she had no comprehensible basis for her action.

> O God! a beast, that wants discourse of reason
> Would have mourn'd longer. . . .
>
> (I. II. 150–1)

And, as is implicit in his initial longing for death, he knows that his is a totally frustrating position, for though he clearly sees the evil, he can find no valid response to it.

> It is not, nor it cannot come to good.
> But break, my heart, for I must hold my tongue!
>
> (I. II. 158–9)

In this, his first appearance alone on the stage, Hamlet, before he has an inkling that he might soon be provided with a motive for action, concerns himself largely with the problem of motivation. He longs for suicide, but that is forbidden. He has seen his mother commit an act for which no motive comprehensible in human, rational terms can be discovered. Just after he sees the Ghost, Hamlet is alone briefly on the stage, and he thinks that he has found a valid basis for action.

> O all you host of heaven! O earth! What else?
> And shall I couple hell? O, fie! Hold, hold, my heart!
> And you, my sinews, grow not instant old,
> But bear me stiffly up. Remember thee?
> Ay, thou poor ghost, whiles memory holds a seat
> In this distracted globe. Remember thee?
> Yea, from the table of my memory
> I'll wipe away all trivial fond records,
> All saws of books, all forms, all pressures past
> That youth and observation copied there,
> And thy commandment all alone shall live
> Within the book and volume of my brain,
> Unmix'd with baser matter.
>
> (I. v. 92–104)

Laertes' first response to his father's death is expressed in exactly the same terms. He, too, abandons all other considerations, sends allegiance, vows, conscience, and grace 'to the profoundest pit', dares damnation, and gives 'both the worlds . . . to negligence' in order to be revenged 'most thoroughly' for his father. Laertes perseveres. Hamlet, however, in his next soliloquy is made to consider the nature of all human actions and the validity of the various bases on which it can rest, here with particular reference to the problem of revenge. The player's response to Hecuba is, apparently, real and unequivocal; yet Hecuba, the basis of his response, is nothing, a straw.

> Is it not monstrous that this player here,
> But in a fiction, in a dream of passion,
> Could force his soul so to his own conceit
> That, from her working all his visage wann'd,
> Tears in his eyes, distraction in's aspect,
> A broken voice, and his whole function suiting
> With forms to his conceit? And all for nothing!
> For Hecuba!
> What's Hecuba to him, or he to Hecuba,
> That he should weep for her?
>
> (II. ii. 535–44)

Hecuba, that is, serves the player in exactly the same way that the little patch of ground serves Fortinbras; neither has any inherent validity, yet each man allows himself to act by assigning value to the object of his action. This is clearly a circular process; the object has no inherent validity which will permit action, yet it is given validity because action is devoted to its cause. Hamlet, as he later does when considering Fortinbras' example, here distinguishes between his object and that of the player.

> What would he do,
> Had he the motive and the cue for passion
> That I have? He would drown the stage with tears
> And cleave the general ear with horrid speech. . . .
> Yet I,
> A dull and muddy-mettled rascal, peak
> Like John-a-dreams, unpregnant of my cause,
> And can say nothing! No, not for a king,
> Upon whose property and most dear life
> A damn'd defeat was made.

(II. II. 544–56)

He consequently derides himself for not being able to act when he has a motive, seeing before him a man who can act with no motive at all. But Shakespeare checks Hamlet's self-abuse, at line 568, and turns him back to his careful and reasonable plan to test Claudius' guilt; he knows, however clear his motives for action might seem, that things are not always as they seem. His mother's marriage, Ophelia's apparent rejection of him, and Rosencrantz' and Guildenstern's apparent betrayal all contribute to the frustrating world he inhabits, but that 'things rank and gross in nature' possess the world does not necessarily mean that Claudius is among those things. The Ghost might be.

> The spirit that I have seen
> May be the devil; and the devil hath power
> T' assume a pleasing shape; yea, and perhaps
> Out of my weakness and my melancholy,
> As he is very potent with such spirits,
> Abuses me to damn me. I'll have grounds
> More relative than this. The play's the thing
> Wherein I'll catch the conscience of the King.

(II. II. 584–91)

Laertes never questions the validity of what he considers to be his natural and honourable duty; consequently he 'dare[s] damnation' on very slender grounds, and is destroyed. Hamlet is here made aware of the danger, and refuses to be so easily tricked into an action that may be damnable.

Hamlet's next soliloquy (III. 1. 56–90), the 'To be, or not to be' soliloquy, follows the previous one by only a few minutes. Whatever other contribution the speech might be presumed to make, it clearly serves not as a resolution to action but as a climax to the search for valid bases for action in which Hamlet has been engaged during the first two acts of the play. The soliloquies of those two acts particularize his search in terms of the various kinds of action which are apparently demanded of him; this soliloquy generalizes the search, and Hamlet contemplates the two contexts in which a basis for action in general, if it is to be found at all, must be found: what we can know of this life, and what we can know of the next. The issue, for Hamlet, is to discover if either of these contexts can afford a basis for action. What he knows – and what the audience has been shown – of 'being' is discouraging. This world includes 'The slings and arrows of outrageous fortune', and it is beset by 'a sea of troubles'. Is it 'nobler in the mind to suffer' these things, Hamlet debates with himself, or 'by opposing end them'? 'Outrageous fortune' and the 'sea of troubles' are to Hamlet so inevitably a part of this world – of 'being' – that to end them is 'to die – to sleep'. This is neither a contemplation of suicide nor a realization that action against the King involves mortal danger for himself. Hamlet merely sees 'outrageous fortune' as a necessary condition of this world. Consequently, one cannot live in this world and free himself from outrageous fortune; the one implies the other. The other world, the state referred to by Hamlet's 'not to be', is appealing largely because it offers relief from outrageous fortune.

> No more; and by a sleep to say we end
> The heartache and the thousand natural shocks
> That flesh is heir to. 'Tis a consummation
> Devoutly to be wish'd.
>
> (III. 1. 61–4)

But this too, as a context in which one might find a basis for action, offers problems. It is inscrutable.

> To sleep – perchance to dream: ay, there's the rub!
> For in that sleep of death what dreams may come
> When we have shuffled off this mortal coil,
> Must give us pause. There's the respect
> That makes calamity of so long life.

(III. 1. 65–9)

The debate is consequently an insoluble one, for though fortune in this world remains outrageous, ignorance and, consequently, fear of the next world prevent any action which would remove us from subjection to this fortune.

> For who would bear the whips and scorns of time,
> Th' oppressor's wrong, the proud man's contumely,
> The pangs of despis'd love, the law's delay,
> The insolence of office, and the spurns
> That patient merit of th' unworthy takes,
> When he himself might his quietus make
> With a bare bodkin? Who would fardels bear,
> To grunt and sweat under a weary life,
> But that the dread of something after death –
> The undiscover'd country, from whose bourn
> No traveller returns – puzzles the will,
> And makes us rather bear those ills we have
> Than fly to others that we know not of?

(III. 1. 70–82)

This soliloquy differs from the earlier ones partly in that it makes no reference to the particular course of action, revenge, which circumstances have urged on Hamlet. It is instead an elemental debate examining whether there be a context in which it is proper and possible for man to act. Hamlet discovers that he cannot know. For, just as rigourously as he maintains the inscrutability of the next world, he maintains the conviction that a necessary condition of this world is 'outrageous fortune', a context in which no meaningful action is possible.

> Thus conscience does make cowards of us all,
> And thus the native hue of resolution
> Is sicklied o'er with the pale cast of thought,
> And enterprises of great pitch and moment

With this regard their currents turn awry,
And lose the name of action.

(III. i. 83–8)

It is useful to remember that the Hamlet who can find no generally valid basis of action is the Hamlet who, in terms of his particular call to action, has not yet determined to his satisfaction Claudius' guilt. Before Hamlet discovers Claudius to be guilty of killing King Hamlet, much of Hamlet's energy, and much of the energy of the play, is spent in detecting that guilt. He does not have to choose a course of action beyond the detective effort, for he has yet to prove Claudius guilty. But when he does prove, to his satisfaction, the King's guilt, a much more basic dilemma is presented to him. Grant Claudius guilty, and the basic question becomes this: is Claudius' guilt a valid basis for Hamlet's contemplated revenge? If rigorously extended to this particular, the general conclusions of the 'To be, or not to be' soliloquy forbid action, for the contexts in which man must act are so inscrutable as to render the motives of all action suspect at best. When Shakespeare confronts Hamlet with the opportunity of killing Claudius, he makes the dilemma precisely the same.

Shakespeare, clearly, need not have included any opportunity for Hamlet to kill Claudius this early in the play. Nothing subsequently occurs which could not have occurred if the prayer scene had not been written. If Shakespeare had moved Hamlet directly from his baiting of Rosencrantz and Guildenstern following the play-within-the-play to his mother's bed-chamber, the play's course could have run smoothly on.[6] It seems therefore useless to speculate about why Hamlet fails to kill Claudius here.[7] The question is why Shakespeare included the scene at all, since, granted the existence of the scene, the reason Shakespeare gives Hamlet for his decision is clear enough. He thinks killing Claudius at that moment would send Claudius to heaven; sending Claudius to heaven for killing King Hamlet would be 'hire and salary, not revenge'. Although the scene contributes nothing to the narrative, however, and although Hamlet's professed reasons for sparing Claudius may or may not be out of character, the scene does contribute one, most significant piece to the dramatic pattern. It puts into action the numbing conclusions of Hamlet's 'To be, or not to be' soliloquy. There Hamlet had concluded that though fortune in this world is outrageous, the dread of the inscrutable 'something after death/ ... puzzles the will'. Yet in his speech on seeing Claudius defenceless, a speech which Shakespeare frames with Claudius' distinction between 'the corrupted currents of this world' and heavenly justice, Hamlet, depending on evidence acquired only from 'our circumstance and course of thought', acts as though the ways of salvation and damnation were infinitely clear to him. Universal justification for human action remains, as the play has developed the idea, beyond man's reach, and Hamlet's mistaken assumption, here, that he has grasped it marks the climax of his frustrating quest.

In the bedroom scene, after this climactic moment, Shakespeare recalls the beginnings of Hamlet's inquiry into the values of his world by emphasizing again Hamlet's incredulity that Gertrude could move from King Hamlet to Claudius. Since not even sense, and certainly not judgment, could 'on this fair mountain leave to feed,/ And batten on this moor' (III. iv. 66–7), Hamlet can still find no explanation for his mother's behaviour. It is a deed which 'calls virtue hypocrite', and which 'from the body of contraction plucks/ The very soul, and sweet religion makes/ A rhapsody of words!' (III. iv. 42, 46–68). Thus, although his has been a long quest, the Hamlet of the prayer scene and the bedroom scene is not far removed from the anguished and puzzled Hamlet of the first soliloquy, in which the effect of his mother's inexplicable marriage was to cast doubt on the validity of all the norms of rational behaviour. In Hamlet's sudden dispatching of Polonius, the 'wretched, rash, intruding fool', and in Hamlet's demand that Gertrude 'assume a virtue, if you have it not', Shakespeare provides the beginnings of the empirical, nearly fatalistic Hamlet who will enter the play after his return from England, but when we next see Hamlet alone on stage, he is still searching for motives for action which 'godlike reason' can approve. Since he has found none, Hamlet considers Fortinbras' capacity to create a motive out of honour as a most appealing solution to his dilemma.

Honour, however, as Fortinbras displays it and as Hamlet here defines it[8] provides motives for action which are entirely different in kind than those provided by 'godlike reason'. The one subjectively assigns value to permit honourable behaviour; the other discovers objective value to permit virtuous behaviour. It is precisely the issue which Troilus and Hector debate, as E. M. W. Tillyard has remarked, and the two modes of behaviour are defined as being as incompatible here as they are in *Troilus and Cressida*. It is as tempting and as inconceivable that Hamlet should 'find quarrel in a straw/ When honour's at the stake' to resolve the enigmas which his 'godlike reason' has so far failed to penetrate as it had earlier been that he would 'from the table of [his] memory/ . . . wipe away all trivial fond records,/ All saws of books, all forms, all pressures past/ That youth and observation copied there' so that the Ghost's appealing command 'all alone shall live/ Within the book and volume of [his] brain . . .' (I. v. 98–103). Like Hamlet's earlier soliloquies, this one inquires into a motive for action, the conclusions of which inquiry are subsequently found wanting in the baffling world of the play. Hamlet here determines that honour requires that 'from this time forth,/ [His] thoughts be bloody, or be nothing worth' (IV. iv. 65–6). When we next see Hamlet, however, Shakespeare has him realize that the sort of honour Fortinbras represents provides no solution to his dilemma.

The graveyard scene shows us a Hamlet who has learned what Achilles, for instance, in III. iii of *Troilus and Cressida,* fails to understand. The virtue which must not seek remuneration for the thing it was and the honour which is always at the stake can provide a basis for action, but that action, being based on such subjective and shifting values, has no objective or permanent validity. Hamlet sees any action undertaken to gain such honour as futile. Confronted with the abhorrent reminders of mortality which the graveyard provides, Hamlet, a good humanist, considers the two historical figures who have pursued worldly success and honour most successfully, the same figures Robert Ashley pictured to explain the difference, in his simpler world, between true honour and ambition.

> *Ham.* Dost thou think Alexander look'd o' this fashion i' th' earth?
> *Hor.* E'en so.
> *Ham.* And smelt so? Pah!
> *Hor.* E'en so, my lord.
> *Ham.* To what base uses we may return, Horatio! Why may not imagination trace the noble dust of Alexander, till 'a find it stopping a bunghole?
> . . . .
> Imperious Caesar, dead and turn'd to clay,
> Might stop a hole to keep the wind away.
> O, that that earth which kept the world in awe
> Should patch a wall t' expel the winter's flaw!　　(V. i. 184–202)

This is a new Hamlet, one who sees more clearly into the insoluble dilemma which has been plaguing him all the play long. He sees that man's understanding is so limited that he cannot discover if any valid bases for action exist, either in this world or the next, but he also sees that avoiding that dilemma by subjectively assigning a value, such as honour, in order to provide a basis for action is self-defeating. The next scene makes explicit his awareness of man's limited understanding and his awareness of the effect of this limitation on man's action. Hamlet has undertaken an action, sending Rosencrantz and Guildenstern to their death, and, explaining that action to Horatio, he makes it clear not only that he undertook to act only in direct response to a very specific problem – he discovered Claudius' letter ordering his death in England – but also that even within this context his actions were not altogether the result of his own choice; his first motions were 'rash', and some other power was operating on him as well. His spontaneous stabbing of Polonius, and his ascribing that act to heaven's having 'pleas'd it so . . ./ That I must be their scourge and minister', is the forerunner of his sending Rosencrantz and Guildenstern to their death, and, as there, so here he denies any larger, preconceived motive for his act.

> Sir, in my heart there was a kind of fighting
> That would not let me sleep. Methought I lay
> Worse than the mutines in the bilboes. Rashly –
> And prais'd be rashness for it; let us know,
> Our indiscretion sometimes serves us well
> When our deep plots do pall; and that should learn us
> There's a divinity that shapes our ends,
> Rough-hew them how we will. . . .
> Up from my cabin . . .
> Grop'd I to find out them. . . .

>   (V. II. 4–14)

After this first deed was undertaken, Hamlet insists, he acted in simple self-defence. He is not responsible for the deaths of Rosencrantz and Guildenstern; they had made the prior choice and are responsible for the consequences of that choice.

> Why, man, they did make love to this employment!
> They are not near my conscience; their defeat
> Does by their own insinuation grow.

'Tis dangerous when the baser nature comes
Between the pass and fell incensed points
Of mighty opposites.

(V. II. 57–62)

But the telling addition, in this scene, is Hamlet's idea that 'there's a divinity that shapes our ends'. The idea is further developed, though briefly, in a later speech, which Shakespeare includes though it has only trivial relevance to the narrative. 'How was [the letter] seal'd?' Horatio asks. 'Even in that was heaven ordinant' (V. II. 47–8), Hamlet replies. The divinity which shapes our ends and the heaven which provided Hamlet with the seal remains, at least in the description of his action regarding Rosencrantz and Guildenstern, vaguely defined. Hamlet does not assume any knowledge of this power; he merely reflects on the possibility of its influence. But there remains the problem of Claudius, and the scene next directs Hamlet's new understanding to his 'mighty opposite'. Hamlet has by now abandoned all thought of justifying revenge by reference to eternal reward and damnation; Hamlet carefully limits his motives to those things he believes he can know.

Does it not, think thee, stand me now upon –
He that hath kill'd my king and whor'd my mother;
Popp'd in between th' election and my hopes;
Thrown out his angle for my proper life,
And with such coz'nage – is't not perfect conscience
To quit him with this arm? And is't not to be damn'd
To let this canker of our nature come
In further evil?

(V. II. 63–70)

The rhetoric of this passage is revealing. No doubt is implied that Claudius has killed the King, whored Gertrude, and tried to deprive Hamlet of both life and throne, nor is there doubt implied that he is a 'canker' of nature, one of the things rank and gross which had so afflicted Hamlet's understanding of his world at the beginning of the play. Hamlet's proper response, however, is not so clear. It is posed interrogatively, for, though Claudius is clearly guilty, the basis of all action is finally inscrutable, and to assume otherwise would be to delude one's self.

A few lines later in the same scene, Shakespeare brings Hamlet's quest among the inscrutable values of his world to its logical conclusion. Challenged by Horatio to obey his mind if it 'dislike any thing', Hamlet refuses.

> *Ham.* Not a whit, we defy augury; there's a special providence in the fall of a sparrow. If it be now, 'tis not to come; if it be not to come, it will be now; if it be not now, yet it will come: the readiness is all. Since no man knows aught of what he leaves, what is't to leave betimes? Let be.
>
> (V. II. 205–10)

No man can know anything about this life, about the connection between this life and 'providence', or about the life to come. Consequently, to try to find a basis for action in any but the most limited of contexts – such as Hamlet's sending Rosencrantz and Guildenstern to their death – is futile. Hamlet does not even choose to take up the King's wager. 'I will walk here in the hall', Shakespeare has Hamlet respond to Osric's announcement of the duel. 'If it please his Majesty, it is the breathing time of day with me. Let the foils be brought, the gentlemen willing, and the King hold his purpose, I will win for him if I can ...' (V. II. 165–8). Within this severely limited context we finally see that there is no answer to Hamlet's 'To be, or not to be'. Since both conditions are inscrutable, since the conventional forms of behaviour required by obedience, honour, and love are untrustworthy guides in this world, and since assigning value to a cause in order to salvage honour from life provides a merely apparent and transitory solution, there remains only the fatalistic 'readiness' to meet whatever circumstance 'outrageous fortune' or 'the divinity that shapes our ends' might provide. Hamlet does not adhere to his early and morally anarchic 'There is nothing either good or bad but thinking makes it so' (II. II. 245–6). That is Troilus' code, but basic to *Hamlet* is the assumption that there may exist an ideal, objective, and permanent system of moral value which if man could but know it would serve as a valid basis of his, consequently, virtuous actions. Hamlet achieves his tragic stature in large part because, having rejected the invalid and misleading standards of behaviour which Ophelia, Laertes, and Fortinbras accept, and having assumed the existence of a divinity which shapes our ends, he recognizes the frustrating distance between what reality is and what we can know of it.

Notes to Chapter 5

[1] E. M. W. Tillyard, *Shakespeare's Problem Plays* (London, 1951), has noted the similarity between the issue debated by the Trojan council and Hamlet's soliloquy in response to hearing the captain describe Fortinbras' wars. 'Helen', Tillyard remarks, 'in the Trojan council has exactly the same position as the barren piece of land in Hamlet's questionings: her final justification is that she is an argument of honour ...' (p. 79).

[2] Theodore Spencer, *Shakespeare and the Nature of Man* (New York, 1961), p. 94.

[3] Siegel (p. 130) notes that James Cleland's courtesy book, *The Institution of a Young Noble Man*, comments on the practice of referring to experts' judgments about honour in the case of an affront. Siegel thinks Cleland's comment is satirical, a judgment which may be affected by his contention that courtesy books expound the 'Christian humanist ideal of honour' whereas duelling treatises expound the 'neo-chivalric cult of honour'. In any case, Cleland's book, whatever its tone, and such treatises as Segar's *The Booke of Honor and Armes* (1590) demonstrate that such an appeal to authority as Laertes proposes was conventionally considered an appropriate step in the formal preservation of honour.

[4] See above, pp. 17–18. Romei, in another part of *The Courtiers Academie*, had Gualinguo argue that 'a woman ... as in many other things, so in [being unchaste] is of harder condition than a man'. He lists four reasons for thinking so, the last of which is that if guilty of adultery, 'a woman offendeth extreamely against her owne proper and principall vertue, which is honestie' (p. 97).

[5] The scene has occasioned three different kinds of critical response. John Dover Wilson, in *What Happens in Hamlet* (New York, 1959; Cambridge, 1951), offers a textual solution: the Second Quarto and the First Folio, he argues, omit a stage direction for Hamlet to enter at II.ii.150, which entrance would permit his hearing Polonius' 'I'll loose my daughter to him' (pp. 101 ff.). Whitaker, in *Shakespeare's Use of Learning*, argues that Shakespeare's failure to provide Hamlet with a motive is a 'loose end' left over from his re-arrangement of his earlier version of the play (p. 261; see also pp. 329–46). Theodore Spencer, in *Shakespeare and the Nature of Man*, is the most persuasive of the critics who argue that Shakespeare has in fact provided Hamlet with a motive. 'Hamlet throughout the play can think of the relations between the sexes only in the coarsest terms; he tortures both Ophelia and himself by doing so, attributing to her in his usual generalizing way the faults of her sex as a whole which his mother's behaviour had revealed' (p. 105).

⁶ Polonius' hypothetically impossible speed in scampering from the hall of the castle at the end of III. ii to Gertrude's bedroom at the beginning of III.iv has bothered readers concerned with the realistically probable. If it had bothered Shakespeare he probably would not have re-introduced Polonius into III.ii for the five lines of dialogue he delivers at the end of that scene, and omitting Polonius there seems the only narrative accommodation that omitting the prayer scene might require.

⁷ William Farnham, in his introduction to the Pelican Edition of the play, neatly displays the puzzlement that has greeted this scene. 'For some reason (we ourselves never stop testing to find it)', Farnham remarks, '[Hamlet] loses at this moment of opportunity all truth he has won about revenge as a crying *immediate* need'. *The Complete Works* (Baltimore, 1969), p. 932.

⁸ See above, pp. 91–2.

Chapter 6

OTHELLO
An Honourable Murderer

> *Lodovico*: O thou Othello that wert once so good,
>   Fall'n in the practice of a damned slave,
>   What shall be said to thee?
> *Othello*:   Why, anything:
>   An honourable murderer, if you will;
>   For naught I did in hate, but all in honour.
>
> (V. II. 291–5)

An irony which is fundamental to *Othello*, but which has been generally overlooked, is expressed in these lines. Since the middle of Act III Othello has been possessed by the idea that if Desdemona be adulterous honour requires that he kill her. This assumption and the circumstances which nurture its existence are the bases of the tragedy. Iago is able to make Othello jealous by deluding him about the facts, a delusion whose probability the play may or may not be concerned to protect, but a kind of delusion that is, in itself, not tragic. Desdemona's innocence, like, for instance, Cordelia's, is a given of the narrative and renders the tragedy more poignant, partly by clarifying the poetic justice according to which Othello meets his end, but it is only the occasion, not the basis, of the tragedy. Shakespeare provides that basis by having the theretofore virtuous Othello succumb, in III. III, to the idea that the affront to his honour requires revenge; he thereby sets Othello on much the same sort of tragic course he had established for Brutus, for if Othello obeys to the letter the code of behaviour he is made to adopt, he can reach only self-destructive and tragic ends. The structure of *Julius Caesar* differs from that of *Othello* in that Brutus is presented from the outset as having an enigmatic but compelling commitment to 'the name of honour'. The Othello of the first two-

and-a-half acts is the picture of a virtuous man precisely aware of the conventionally appropriate relationship between that virtue and the honour it gains him; in III. III he is made to succumb to an entirely different, and equally recognizable, idea about the nature of honour, and this fundamental change in his moral allegiances is at the heart of the tragedy.

The importance to the theme and structure of the play of Othello's ironic appeal to honour to justify his action has probably been overlooked because of the two most puzzling difficulties which the complexity of the play has imposed on post-Shakespearean or post-Restoration readers. First, the Othello of the first half of the play behaves in an entirely different manner than the Othello of the last half. Second, a major part of the narrative interest of the play, Iago's misleading Othello, is apparently not so successfully bonded with the basic concern of the play, the nature of Othello's tragic error, as in the other mature tragedies.[1] Neither of these, in all likelihood, provided a dilemma for Shakespeare's own audience. In the first instance, the play clearly depends on what were common Renaissance assumptions about honour to explain Othello's tragic reversal in III. III. In the second, the same commonplace assumptions about honour would have made evident the similarity between Iago's initial motives and Othello's later, debased ones, so the basic structure of the play is a familiar dramatic artifice. Iago foreshadows the error into which Othello will fall. Shakespeare does not develop this parallel into an elaborate sub-plot, and, to be sure, Iago is the antagonist and villain rather than a strictly parallel character, like Gloucester, but the principle of dramatizing a basic theme of a play in two different characters or sets of characters is familiar; Fortinbras, Ophelia, and Laertes, for instance, are made to act out the consequences of actions which Shakespeare has Hamlet consider, but resist. To argue, with E. E. Stoll, that Othello 'becomes jealous through "a mechanical device", the conventional idea that the slanderer is always believed', may be to reduce the play merely to mechanics, but it is quite another matter to see Iago, as villain, foreshadowing and suffering from the error into which Othello will tragically fall. Important aspects of the basic structure of the play reside in this parallel; Othello, initially presented as a man whose concern for honour is, appropriately, subsidiary to and derivative from the various virtues he is given to possess, is in Act III and thereafter reduced to dependence on the debased forms of honour which Iago represents from the outset.[2]

The idea that a cuckold is justified in taking his revenge – even to the point of murder – on both his faithless wife and her lover has a long history, and in some quarters is no doubt still given credit. In Shakespeare's day the idea was more precisely formulated, or at least more often formulated, because it was made an integral part of Renaissance speculations about honour. This identification of the idea with honour has been widely documented in recent times, both by reference to tracts on honour and to the great number of plays of the time which identify revenge for adultery with the demands of honour.[3] Indeed in the story of the jealous Moor which Shakespeare took from Giraldi Cinthio there is never any doubt that adultery requires such revenge; the point of Cinthio's account is that Desdemona is unjustly murdered because she is chaste. In a revealing paragraph which describes the outcome of the affair, Cinthio exhibits a convoluted idea of honour and justice which can at once recognize the social stigma attached to a Venetian's being killed by a barbarian, admire the Moor's courage in not confessing the truth under torture, praise Desdemona's relatives for exacting private revenge, and – most tellingly – condemn the Moor's act only because his jealousy was unwarranted.

> The villain testified that ... the Moor had told him everything and had even tried to induce him to commit both crimes, and that having finally killed his wife himself out of bestial and unwarranted jealousy, the Moor had told him of the manner in which he killed her. The authorities, on hearing of this crime by a barbarian against one of their citizens, had the Moor arrested in Cyprus and brought to Venice, where they tried by torture to wring the truth out of him. He, however, courageously withstood the pain and denied everything so resolutely that nothing could be drawn from him. But although he escaped death through his steadfastness, he was, after many days in prison, condemned to perpetual exile, where he was finally killed by Desdemona's kinsfolk as he deserved.[4]

Shakespeare gives this commonplace assumption that honour requires that adultery be revenged to most of the characters in *Othello*, but we oversimplify the play and do a disservice to the quality of Shakespeare's thought if we consequently assume that he accepts this commonplace as valid and does not question it in the play. One of the differences between Shakespeare's play and Cinthio's moral tale is that *Othello* dramatizes the Moor's jealous act, and his tragedy, as being the consequences of obedience to the compelling demands of honour.

At the beginning of the play we are made aware that the attitude towards honour which Iago represents is the precise obverse of Othello's. The play begins with Iago's announcing one of the reasons he hates Othello; 'his Moorship' has preferred Cassio, a mere theoretician, to Iago, whose worth has been proved, he announces, in practice. The play is clearly not concerned with the question of who is in fact the better soldier, or with the question of whether Iago has indeed been wronged; it is concerned to provide, in this expository scene, for Iago's hatred of Othello. This speech provides an affront Iago considers his honour as a soldier to have suffered, and Shakespeare makes it a familiar affront by having Iago complain in terms that a Jacobean audience would immediately recognize. He considers himself to have proved his worth 'At Rhodes, at Cyprus, and on other grounds/ Christian and heathen' (I. i. 29–30), and he expects the honourable reward which that worth should engender. But although 'three great ones of the city . . ./ Off-capp'd to him', and although Iago considers himself to be 'worth no less a place' (I. i. 8–11), Othello has chosen Cassio. The affront to his honour as a soldier is further intensified by his rival's being, in his view, merely an 'arithmetician', a man who 'never set a squadron in the field' (I. i. 22). Ulysses, it may be recalled, knew that the mighty Achilles and his disrespectful friend 'mock our policy and call it cowardice', and Hotspur's attitude towards his popinjay provides the comic extreme of the soldier's idea that honour can only be won in actual combat. Iago's speech provides straightforward exposition, if the urge to speculate on such hypothetical matters prior to the play as the validity of Iago's charge be curtailed; Iago thinks his honour as a soldier has been affronted, and he wants revenge. Each of the actions and speeches which Shakespeare gives Iago in this act shows us an Iago trying to put his revenge in motion, and in the concluding speech of the act another reason for Iago's hatred of Othello is provided; he announces that his honour as a husband has also been affronted.

> I hate the Moor;
> And it is thought abroad that 'twixt my sheets

'Has done my office: I know not if't be true;
Yet I, for mere suspicion in that kind,
Will do as if for surety.

(I. III. 378–82)

In both cases the emphasis which Shakespeare has Iago give to his complaints makes the contrast with Othello pronounced. Iago, by acting according to what 'is thought abroad' and for revenge at having been denied the mark of honour which the lieutenancy represents, rather than being concerned to provide service to the state or with the truth of Emilia's supposed unfaithfulness, provides an exact inversion of the virtuous principles to which Othello is made to adhere. Othello, too, is characterized as a soldier and a husband in this expository act, and Shakespeare is careful to make him virtuous in both roles and to make his understanding of the honour appropriate to those roles older, orthodox, and ultimately Aristotelian. Robert Ashley could be describing the Othello of the first act, so perfectly virtuous and therefore honourable has Shakespeare drawn his noble Moor.

Whiles we endevour therfore after true honour, all kind of ostenta-cion ys to be eschewed. . . . Hence appeareth that they are all to blame which commend their own lynage or wealth, or learning or any other good thing in themselves.[5]

The similarity of this idea with the speech in which Shakespeare has Othello explain his motives for marrying is marked, and it was so commonplace an idea in orthodox statements about honour that Shakespeare must have found it dramatically useful in his effort to present the perfectly virtuous and therefore, from the orthodox point of view, perfectly honourable man. In his role both as soldier and husband, Othello is made precisely aware of the virtuous course, and Shakespeare, by introducing Othello's royal heritage, defines Othello's virtue as being untainted by ambition or any of the other temptations to which the orthodox man of honour was considered subject. Giving Othello this royal heritage serves no other apparent purpose, so when Shakespeare has Iago warn that Brabantio will exert all his power to separate Desdemona and Othello, Othello's response was in all likeli-hood designed to present him to the audience as a perfect instance of the sort of honourable man which Ashley's definition so neatly describes.

> Let him do his spite.
> My services which I have done the signiory
> Shall outtongue his complaints. 'Tis yet to know –
> Which, when I know that boasting is an honour,
> I shall promulgate – I fetch my life and being
> From men of royal siege; and my demerits
> May speak unbonneted to as proud a fortune
> As this that I have reach'd. For know, Iago,
> But that I love the gentle Desdemona,
> I would not my unhoused free condition
> Put into circumscription and confine
> For the sea's worth.
>
> (I. II. 17–28)

The service he has done is his soldiership, and he is confident of the worth of that, an easy enough virtue for Shakespeare to introduce here and to expand in the council scene. But the marriage has to be made virtuous too, and the addition of Othello's royal heritage serves the purpose; since he is pursuing no selfish ends, he is presented as a man with the purest of motives. Shakespeare also makes him precisely aware of the sort of honourable demand for moderation that Ashley had recorded, and so completes the characterization, in Othello's first speech of any length, of his protagonist as a soldier and husband who is precisely aware of the honour appropriate to his virtues. When Iago urges flight, Othello stands firm on his worth.

> Not I. I must be found.
> My parts, my title, and my perfect soul
> Shall manifest me rightly.
>
> (I. II. 30–2)

When Brabantio appears, Shakespeare has Othello remain more than merely calm; he makes him respond to Brabantio in terms of the widespread idea that the different roles men play require different sorts of virtuous action.

> Keep up your bright swords, for the dew will rust them.
> Good signior, you shall more command with years
> Than with your weapons.
>
> (I. II. 59–61)

And Othello accurately distinguishes between Brabantio's quite inappropriate use of force and the use of law to resolve the matter.

> Hold your hands,
> Both you of my inclining, and the rest.
> Were it my cue to fight, I should have known it
> Without a prompter. Where will you that I go
> To answer this your charge?
>
> (I. II. 81–5)

Borrowing Othello's metaphor, one notices that the important difference between Othello and the other characters in this act is that, though Othello chooses his actions, the other characters obey their cues like players. This marionette-like response is obvious in Brabantio and Roderigo; Iago prompts their actions by appealing to their passions. Iago, too, is prompted by jealousy and revenge. Only Othello, this far in Act I, is shown able to act 'without a prompter', and he consistently chooses the virtuous course.

The other scene of Act I in which Othello appears is set in the council chamber, in the presence of the Duke and Senators. This is an efficient expository scene, for it introduces Desdemona, has Othello answer Brabantio's charge, and moves the action towards Cyprus; late in the scene, Shakespeare again turns explicitly to the terms which frame the entire play. The narrative necessity of getting Desdemona to Cyprus is put to thematic use when Othello assures the Senators that there can be no conflict between his duties as a soldier and his role as a husband. He first defends his motives:

> Let her have your voices.
> Vouch with me heaven, I therefore beg it not
> To please the palate of my appetite . . .
> But to be free and bounteous to her mind.
>
> (I. III. 260–5)

Shakespeare has him expand this by explaining what the consequences of allowing his love to compromise his soldierly duty would be. His awareness of these consequences and his intention to prevent them are from an orthodox point of view again exact; his primary concern is with his duty – i.e. his virtue – and he knows that failure to perform that duty will result in a loss of honour. This is conspicuously a different manner of thinking of honour than as a justification for revenge.

And heaven defend your good souls that you think
I will your serious and great business scant
For she is with me. No, when light-wing'd toys
Of feather'd Cupid seel with wanton dullness
My speculative and offic'd instruments,
That my disports corrupt and taint my business,
Let housewives make a skillet of my helm,
And all indign and base adversities
Make head against my estimation!

(I. iii. 266–74)

This is heavily ironic, of course, but Othello's explicit statement keeps a strictly orthodox balance between virtue and the loss of honour which would attend his failure to perform the virtuous acts required by his soldiership. We have only to compare Othello's intention here, to pursue the Venetian Senators' 'great business', with Iago's anger at missing the lieutenancy and his intention to act according to what 'is thought abroad' to realize what definition the first act makes of the two chief characters. Shakespeare establishes both in the roles of soldier and husband, and gives them precisely opposite assumptions about the virtuous requirements of those roles and about the honour which theoretically should attend them. Consequently, we have an antagonist who, though he is pictured as able to manipulate the actions of men by appealing to their passions, is himself in the grip of a rigid commitment to revenge his affronted honour, and a protagonist who, apparently his polar opposite, is virtuous and honourable according to the most orthodox and optimistic uses of the terms.

Shakespeare maintains this balance in the second act. The witty and disruptive Iago is kept before us, generally misogynous, particularly sure that the 'courtesy' which Roderigo sees in the dialogue between Desdemona and Cassio is 'lechery, by this hand', and still led on to 'diet [his] revenge' (II. ii. 252–3, 258) for Emilia's supposed adultery.

For that I do suspect the lusty Moor
Hath leap'd into my seat; the thought whereof
Doth, like a poisonous mineral, gnaw my inwards. . . .

(II. i. 289–91)

Shakespeare juxtaposes Othello's entry into the scene and loving welcome to Desdemona with Iago's cynical scheming and witty but malevolent dialogue with Desdemona in dispraise of women. Othello's entrance is expressed in hyperbolic terms, in which there is again a good deal of dramatic irony, but they are terms which mark a clear contrast between Othello's and Iago's attitude towards women and towards marriage.

> O my soul's joy!
> If after every tempest come such calms,
> May the winds blow till they have waken'd death!
> ... If it were now to die,
> 'Twere now to be most happy; for I fear
> My soul hath her content so absolute
> That not another comfort like to this
> Succeeds in unknown fate.

(II. I. 182–91)

The contrast between the two as husbands is thus maintained in the first scene of the act; after the brief proclamation which comprises the second scene, Shakespeare returns to their roles as soldiers, and to the two, contradictory attitudes towards honour which they have come to represent.

The drunken brawl which costs Cassio his lieutenancy and plays so neatly into Iago's hand is drawn from a brief note in Cinthio that 'the Moor had occasion to demote the Captain for having wounded a soldier while on sentry duty'.[6] It serves Shakespeare efficiently and well, for by means of this incident he is able not only to put into action the contrast between Iago's and Othello's soldiership which the expository speeches of Act I introduce, but also to develop a pattern of action in Cassio which prefigures precisely, though in small, the tragic reversal Othello will undergo in the following act.

Othello is, throughout, made the picture of the perfect commander. The brawl and its aftermath are necessary to the narrative, but the beginning of the scene serves no apparent purpose other than the characterization of Othello which it provides. Though the revels are a celebration, Othello knows that decorum and honour must be maintained.

> Good Michael, look you to the guard to-night.
> Let's teach ourselves that honourable stop,
> Not to outsport discretion.

(II. III. 1–3)

121

And side by side with this, Shakespeare makes him still the husband; secure in his love and perfect in his duty, he is the perfectly balanced man.

> Come, my dear love.
> The purchase made, the fruits are to ensue;
> That profit's yet to come 'tween me and you.
>
> (II. III. 8–10)

When Othello, some 170 lines later, enters upon the brawl which Iago's constant effort for revenge has constructed, he is the voice of order and reason – even Christian Reason.

> Are we turn'd Turks, and to ourselves do that
> Which heaven hath forbid the Ottomites?
> For Christian shame put by this barbarous brawl!
> He that stirs next to carve for his own rage
> Holds his soul light; he dies upon his motion.
> Silence that dreadful bell! It frights the isle
> From her propriety. What's the matter, masters?
>
> (II. III. 153–9)

He gets no answer, and turns to Montano for one. The assumptions about virtue and honour in his question are strictly orthodox and strictly consistent with the Othello defined by the first act.

> Worthy Montano, you were wont be civil;
> The gravity and stillness of your youth
> The world hath noted, and your name is great
> In mouths of wisest censure. What's the matter
> That you unlace your reputation thus
> And spend your rich opinion for the name
> Of a night-brawler? Give me answer to't.
>
> (II. III. 173–9)

Montano's virtue, Othello correctly points out, is the result of his having moderated the natural tendency towards extreme behaviour to which youth is subject, a familiar enough part of orthodox moral speculations. The same attitude towards the difficulties in the way of youthful virtue is reflected in Hector's response to Paris and Troilus that they have argued 'not much/ Unlike young men, who Aristotle thought/ Unfit to hear moral philosophy', for the 'reasons' they have alleged 'do more conduce/ To the hot passion of distemp'red blood/

Than to make up a free determination/ 'Twixt right and wrong . . .'
(II. II. 165–71). Othello is also given the quite orthodox idea that the
consequence of this virtue in Montano is that those wise enough to
comprehend it give him honour. To abandon his moderate, virtuous
course is to abandon the honour that attends it 'for the name/ Of a
night-brawler'. There is no narrative purpose served by this description of Montano, but by dwelling on the brawl Shakespeare expands
his characterization of Othello, a characterization which Othello's
next speech fully develops. Othello seeks the truth so that he may perform the duties required of him as commander.

> Now, by heaven,
> My blood begins my safer guides to rule,
> And passion, having my best judgment collied,
> Assays to lead the way. If I once stir
> Or do but lift this arm, the best of you
> Shall sink in my rebuke. Give me to know
> How this foul rout began, who set it on;
> And he that is approv'd in this offence,
> Though he had twinn'd with me, both at a birth,
> Shall lose me. What! in a town of war,
> Yet wild, the people's hearts brimful of fear,
> To manage private and domestic quarrel?
> In night, and on the court and guard of safety?
> 'Tis monstrous.
>
> (II. III. 187–200)

In a note to this speech, Hardin Craig calls it 'the first indication of
Othello's psychology; he is a man whose judgment may be over-
thrown by his passion'.[7] On the contrary, Othello is made aware of
just such a danger, and is consequently shown to be able to keep his
passion in check; he rejects the show of force to which that passion
tempts him. His proper concern, since he is in command, is with the
town. Thus he announces, in the central portion of the speech, that no
private concerns, even brotherhood, shall intrude on his public duty,
and he shows, in the final portion of the speech, the nature of the
offence. It is 'monstrous' because the officers entrusted to keep order
have themselves introduced disorder. Othello's effort to restore order
is clearly the virtuous course, and thus, though he personally loves
Cassio, he must, as commander, dismiss him.

The first consequence of this brawl is that Cassio considers himself hurt 'past all surgery'. The enormous importance he gives to the reputation – that 'immortal part' of himself – he has lost is a familiar attitude. But there is, once again, no apparent reason of a merely narrative kind for Shakespeare to have developed the aftermath of the brawl in terms of honour. The narrative requires that Cassio sue to Desdemona to intercede for him, but Shakespeare has him reach the decision to make that suit through a process strikingly similar to the process of reversal which he will put Othello through some one hundred lines further into the play. Cassio, like the Othello of the first half of the play, is initially given the orthodox idea that honour can be gained only by virtuous action, and Shakespeare has him reiterate the idea several times; there seems little doubt of the emphasis intended by the scene. He continually rejects the idea of suing to recover his reputation and the lieutenancy, which has been from the outset of the play a convenient mark of the honour Iago thinks he has unjustly lost to Cassio, for he considers his drunkenness to have made him unworthy of it.

> I will rather sue to be despis'd than to deceive so good a commander with so slight, so drunken, and so indiscreet an officer. Drunk? and speak parrot? and squabble? swagger? swear? and discourse fustian with one's own shadow?
>
> (II. III. 259–63)

And in each succeeding speech, until his reversal, Cassio strictly asserts that he cannot ask to have his place restored, for his virtue is at fault. When Iago calls him 'too severe a moraler' and suggests that he 'mend it for [his] own good' (II. III. 279, 282), Cassio knows that such an attempt is futile. Reputation depends on virtue, and his virtue is at fault.

> I will ask him for my place again: he shall tell me I am a drunkard! Had I as many mouths as Hydra, such an answer would stop them all.
>
> (II. III. 283–5)

But suddenly, and inexplicably, Cassio agrees to sue to Desdemona to have his place restored. The contrast could not be more apparent, for he abandons his concern for virtue and makes his choice on the most self-centred and, in comparison with the values he has just been articulating, petty basis imaginable.

> ... Betimes in the morning I will beseech the virtuous
> Desdemona to undertake for me. I am desperate of my fortunes if
> they check me here.
>
> (II. III. 306–8)

Cassio's decision is required by the story line, of course, but by having
the lieutenant suddenly abandon his initial assurance that reputation
and the marks of honour can only be protected by virtuous action,
Shakespeare provides an action parallel to Othello's in III. III. The
consequences of Cassio's reversal are bathetic rather than tragic, but
they do display the moral decay to which he has subjected himself; he
becomes a pathetic currier of favour, and Act III opens with his having
some hired musicians play to Othello to try to win back the regard he
has lost.

> Masters, play here; I will content your pains:
> Something that's brief; and bid 'Good morrow, general.'
>
> (III. I. 1–2)

The play provides no explanation for this sudden change; it merely
dramatizes Cassio's abandoning the way in which he knows virtue lies,
urged on by Iago, to pursue the meaner, self-centred way in which he
thinks the marks of honour lie. In the third scene of Act III, Shakespeare puts Othello through the same sort of reversal.

Shakespeare does not have Othello respond to Iago's insinuations
until relatively late in the scene, and the first speech in which he does
respond represents him as the Othello to whom we have been introduced in the first two acts. He wants to know the truth.

> Think, my lord?
> By heaven, he echoes me,
> As if there were some monster in his thought
> Too hideous to be shown. Thou dost mean something.
> I heard thee say even now, thou lik'st not that,
> When Cassio left my wife. What didst not like?
> And when I told thee he was of my counsel
> In the whole course of wooing, thou cried'st 'Indeed?'
> And didst contract and purse thy brow together,
> As if thou then hadst shut up in thy brain
> Some horrible conceit. If thou dost love me,
> Show me thy thought.
>
> (III. III. 105–16)

Throughout the first part of this extensive dialogue, Shakespeare carefully defines Othello as a man who will not come to unwarranted conclusions. Othello consistently refuses to develop Iago's implications, and demands that Iago be open with him. There is no hint, here, that Othello suspects Iago's purpose or that he is especially subject to jealousy. Indeed, if he were, Iago's hints would be clear enough to him. When Iago says of Cassio, 'I dare be sworn I think that he is honest'. Othello replies, 'I think so too'. When Iago replies, 'men should be what they seem', Othello agrees, 'Certain, men should be what they seem' (III. III. 125–8). Iago finally fails to get Othello to understand his hints, even though he appeals directly to Othello's concern for his reputation.

> *Iago.* Good name in man and woman, dear my lord,
>   Is the immediate jewel of their souls.
>   Who steals my purse steals trash; 'tis something, nothing;
>   'Twas mine, 'tis his, and has been slave to thousands;
>   But he that filches from me my good name
>   Robs me of that which not enriches him
>   And makes me poor indeed.
> *Oth.* By heaven, I'll know thy thoughts!

(III. III. 155–62)

Failing to get Othello to formulate his own conclusion on such scanty grounds, Iago is forced to introduce the idea of jealousy himself. Othello's response, again, is typical of the Othello of the first two acts; he will know the truth and act on it. There is no hint here that he is concerned with his reputation; virtue is at issue.

> Think'st thou I'ld make a life of jealousy,
> To follow still the changes of the moon
> With fresh suspicions? No! To be once in doubt
> Is once to be resolv'd. Exchange me for a goat,
> When I shall turn the business of my soul
> To such exsufflicate and blown surmises,
> Matching thy inference. 'Tis not to make me jealous
> To say my wife is fair, feeds well, loves company,
> Is free of speech, sings, plays, and dances well.
> Where virtue is, these are more virtuous.
> Nor from mine own weak merits will I draw
> The smallest fear or doubt of her revolt,

For she had eyes, and chose me. No Iago;
I'll see before I doubt; when I doubt, prove;
And on the proof there is no more but this –
Away at once with love or jealousy!

(III. III. 177–92)

So Iago is faced with the task of fabricating proof. It is at precisely this point in the play that the relatively unsuccessful bonding of narrative and theme seems most apparent – or, at least, has most puzzled commentators. That Iago dupe Othello is, of course, one of the given circumstances of the play, and jealousy is in the nature of the tale, but that Othello becomes jealous, however passionately, is not his tragic error. The basic error, the moral reversal which will determine his action for the rest of the play, is his henceforward unwavering assumption that since, as he believes, Desdemona is adulterous, he must kill her. This is the basic change in his moral allegiances, for Shakespeare from this moment replaces Othello's perfect virtue and its attendant understanding of the honour appropriately due to him with the same sort of amoral compulsion to revenge the affront to his honour, now understood as independent of and superior to concerns of virtue, that has consistently characterized Iago. If we think of jealousy as Othello's tragic error we have to depend on mere conjecture to see any connection between the Othello of the first two acts and the Othello of the final three, for there is no explicit definition in the early acts of Othello as potentially either jealous or passionately irrational. If, however, we see that jealousy as one of the forces which causes him to abandon the virtuous concerns with which Shakespeare has so carefully provided him for 'honourable' ones of the most debased sort, the artifice of the play becomes more clearly apparent. The first half of the play presents a world of moral absolutes. Othello serves love and duty with actions defined as virtuous and honourable according to the most orthodox ethical notions; Iago serves his own revenge with actions motivated by the most limited and inverted idea of honour available. Othello, in III. III, tragically falls into Iago's world.

Until his temporary exit in the scene, Othello's every word had still been concerned with the moral issue of the guilt at which Iago has been hinting; there is no suggestion that he is merely concerned with the effect of this supposed adultery on his reputation. When he returns, however, he has changed. Iago's speech heralds this change.

> Not poppy nor mandragora,
> Nor all the drowsy syrups of the world,
> Shall ever medicine thee to that sweet sleep
> Which thou ow'dst yesterday.
>
> (III. iii. 330–3)

Othello's first speech announces his reversal; he is no longer concerned with virtue, or with finding the truth so that he may act on it. The façade of virtue is all that he requires.

> Avaunt! be gone! Thou [Iago] hast set me on the rack.
> I swear 'tis better to be much abus'd
> Than but to know't a little.
>
> (III. iii. 335–7)

And his next speech develops the idea fully. This is a crucial speech, for in it Shakespeare reintroduces Othello's role as soldier. The terms in which Othello now thinks of his soldiership are illustrative, for they indicate the sort of change his nature has undergone.

> I had been happy if the general camp,
> Pioneers and all, had tasted her sweet body,
> So I had nothing known. O, now for ever
> Farewell the tranquil mind! farewell content!
> Farewell the plumed troop, and the big wars,
> That make ambition virtue! O, farewell!
> Farewell the neighing steed and the shrill trump,
> The spirit-stirring drum, th' ear-piercing fife,
> The royal banner, and all quality,
> Pride, pomp, and circumstance of glorious war!
> And O you mortal engines, whose rude throats
> Th' immortal Jove's dread clamours counterfeit,
> Farewell! Othello's occupation's gone!
>
> (III. iii. 345–57)

As he has substituted the outward show of virtue for virtue itself in his role as husband, so he has substituted 'pomp' for 'service' in his role as soldier. His regret for 'the big wars,/ That make ambition virtue', recalls Fortinbras' 'divine ambition' and Troilus' inversion of rational principles with his query, 'What is aught, but as 'tis valued?' His earlier concern for the 'service' he has done the state and for his duty as commander is here replaced by a concern for the 'Pride, pomp, and circumstance of glorious war', just as his earlier concern for Desdemona's virtue is here replaced with a willingness to live with the mere façade of her virtue. 'What sense had I of her stol'n hours of lust?' he asks just prior to this speech. 'I saw't not, thought it not, it harm'd not me' (III. III. 338–9).

Most revealing is the difference between the course of action Othello had contemplated when Iago first broached the matter, but before his reversal and the course to which he is driven after his reversal. Early in the scene Othello, still concerned to discover the truth, wonders how Desdemona might have fallen off.

And yet, how nature errring from itself —

(III. III. 227)

Iago interrupts, perverting Othello's meaning to suggest that Desdemona's choice of Othello was an unnatural one, and that her adultery is a repudiation of that unnatural choice.

Ay, there's the point! as (to be bold with you)
Not to affect many proposed matches
Of her own clime, complexion, and degree,
Whereto we see in all things nature tends –
Foh! One may smell in such a will most rank,
Foul disproportion, thoughts unnatural –
But pardon me – I do not in position
Distinctly speak of her; though I may fear
Her will, recoiling to her better judgment,
May fall to match you with her country forms,
And happily repent.

(III. III. 228–38)

But Othello, though beginning to be enmeshed in Iago's web, still views Desdemona's adultery in a context of orthodox morality; he sees her supposed adultery, not her original choice of him, as the unnatural act, and he wonders what might have led her from her nature.

This fellow's [Iago] of exceeding honesty,
And knows all qualities, with a learned spirit
Of human dealings. If I do prove her haggard,

129

Though that her jesses were my dear heartstrings,
I'ld whistle her off and let her down the wind,
To prey at fortune. Haply, for I am black
And have not those soft parts of conversation
That chamberers have, or for I am declin'd
Into the vale of years (yet that's not much),
She's gone. I am abus'd, and my relief
Must be to loathe her. O curse of marriage,
That we can call these delicate creatures ours,
And not their appetites!

(III. III. 258–70)

The response which he here contemplates is strictly consistent with
his earlier character. If Desdemona's 'appetite' has led her so far from
her nature as to make her haggard, then Othello's appropriate response
is to 'loathe her', for if appetite controls her actions, those actions are
according to the precepts of rational morality which govern Othello in
the first half of the play, bestial ones. Indeed, the metaphor Shakespeare chooses indicates that Othello sees such an act as a reversion
to bestiality, and his willingness to 'whistle her off' even though
her jesses were his 'dear heartstrings' is consistent with the sort of
strict adherence to the cause of virtue which had earlier led him to
warn that whoever might be guilty of the 'foul rout' in the watch,
'Though he had twinn'd with me, both at a birth,/ Shall lose me' (II.
III. 195–6). After his reversal, however, Othello is driven to a course of
action which is different in kind, not merely in degree, for he is
far from deciding, 'on the proof', to do 'Away at once with love or
jealousy'.

O, that the slave had forty thousand lives!
One is too poor, too weak for my revenge.
Now do I see 'tis true. Look here, Iago:
All my fond love thus do I blow to heaven.
'Tis gone.
Arise, black vengeance, from thy hollow hell!
Yield up, O love, thy crown and hearted throne
To tyrannous hate! Swell, bosom, with thy fraught,
For 'tis of aspics' tongues!

(III. III. 442–50)

The irony with which Othello is made to blow love 'to heaven' and to call up 'black vengeance' is telling, as his description of hate as tyrannous is accurate, for Othello has abandoned the rational pursuit of virtue for the 'honourable' pursuit of vengeance. His next speech attests to the rigidity of his commitment to vengeance, for he begins by describing his course as so fixed as to be beyond his control, and he ends by making revenge his god.

> Like to the Pontic sea,
> Whose icy current and compulsive course
> Ne'er feels retiring ebb, but keeps due on
> To the Propontic and the Hellespont;
> Even so my bloody thoughts, with violent pace,
> Shall ne'er look back, ne'er ebb to humble love,
> Till that a capable and wide revenge
> Swallow them up. (*He kneels.*) Now, by yond marble heaven,
> In the due reverence of a sacred vow
> I here engage my words.
>
> (III. iii. 453–62)

The moral reversal through which Shakespeare puts Othello is very like, and is as sudden as, the reversal he puts Hector through when he has the Trojan hero abandon the 'moral laws/ Of nature and of nations' for the sake of the Trojans' 'joint and several dignities'. The Moor's falling away from the perfectly virtuous course which had been his is the climactic moment in the play, for after this Shakespeare has him consistently believe that the affront to himself which Desdemona's adultery has caused requires revenge. As Ned B. Allen has pointed out, Shakespeare follows Cinthio much more faithfully in the last part of the play than in the first. Allen believes that 'Shakespeare wrote the two parts . . . at different times – in different frames of mind – and the contradictions between the two parts [are] the result of his having joined them carelessly'.[8] If, however, we grant Shakespeare an interest in his play and the capacity to give it some sort of coherent form, it seems more likely that what Shakespeare has done is make a tragedy of Cinthio's pious reminder that a few women are chaste. At the beginning of the tale Shakespeare added all the details which make Othello the perfectly virtuous man; after his moral reversal, in III. iii, Othello begins to behave as Cinthio's Moor had done – and as, in their various ways, the other characters of the play do. Therein lies the tragedy.

Shakespeare has Lodovico, when he sees Othello strike Desdemona, describe this tragic difference.

> Is this the noble Moor whom our full Senate
> Call all in all sufficient? Is this the nature
> Whom passion could not shake? whose solid virtue
> The shot of accident nor dart of chance
> Could neither graze nor pierce?
>
> (IV. I. 255–9)

'He is much changed', Iago replies, and the final two acts of the play dramatize the consequences and passions of this tragic reversal. Shakespeare keeps Othello's jealousy everpresent, passionate, and severe, but he probes that jealousy and defines its nature and destructive effect by having Othello consistently refer to Desdemona's supposed adultery only in terms of the affront to himself which it represents. It is only in this morally debased context that Desdemona's death is required; just as Shakespeare has Iago in the first act respond only to 'what is thought abroad', so he limits Othello's actions in the final half of the play to those undertaken to revenge the damage done his honour. Helen Gardner, commenting on John Holloway's *The Story of the Night*, considers the effect on modern readers of the demise of 'certain Elizabethan conceptions'. 'We can all accept', she quite rightly argues, 'because it is so wholly dead, the notion of Order and Hierarchy as a universal Law of Nature . . . and find that this gives us a perspective from which to interpret the History Plays'. She distinguishes between such a notion, however, and 'the notion that fidelity is something we look for in those we love, and something we bind ourselves to when we love another person. . . .' This latter, she continues, 'is very much more than an idea which once had validity but is now merely intellectually apprehensible. It is an idea which is still passionately held. . . .'[9] But it is, after all, one thing to expect fidelity in those we love, another to adhere to a widely held and precisely formulated code of behaviour which sees a wife's infidelity chiefly in terms of the dishonour it causes her husband and which requires her death to remove the dishonourable stain. Renaissance speculation about honour does, then, provide an intellectual framework according to which the tragic action of *Othello* may be apprehended as certainly as notions of 'Order and Hierarchy' provide a perspective for the history plays. Othello obeys to the letter the new code he adopts; the tragedy is that he adopted it, and that its tenets are so pervasive that it can never occur to him to question them. Shakespeare has Iago announce and Othello accept the basic idea that only the affront to Othello is at issue.

> *Iago.* If you are so fond over her iniquity, give her patent to offend;
> for, if it touch not you, it comes near nobody.
> *Oth.* I will chop her into messes! Cuckold me!
> *Iago.* O, 'tis foul in her.
> *Oth.* With mine officer!
> *Iago.* That's fouler.

(IV. I. 193–8)

It is only 'fouler' that Cassio should be her lover from the point of view that sees adultery chiefly as an affront to honour and reputation. Shakespeare had Othello, prior to his acceptance of this code, speak of Desdemona's supposed fault in terms of orthodox and rational morality; nature might, he then realized, err from itself. In the grip of the code, Othello swears a 'sacred vow' to accomplish 'a capable and wide revenge' to which the moral issue of Desdemona's supposed guilt is quite irrelevant. 'The service' has, once again, become 'greater than the god', and Othello's delusion remains tragic and absolute.

> An honourable murderer, if you will;
> For naught I did in hate, but all in honour.

(V. II. 294–5)

Notes to Chapter 6

[1] Helen Gardner's excellent survey of the criticism of *Othello* in this century, in '"Othello": A Retrospect, 1900–67', *Shakespeare Survey* 21 (1968), pp. 1–11, first observes that much of the criticism of the play 'has been marked by an uneasiness which was first voiced by Bradley' (p. 1), then describes the major critical responses to the peculiar problems of the play. Hers is an effort to define the relevance to the play of divergent critical opinions. Remarking on E. E. Stoll's 'assault' on Bradley, Professor Gardner argues that Stoll's 'basic contention (that Othello ... becomes insanely jealous through "a mechanical device"; the convention that the slanderer is

always believed) seems less important than the strength of his response to dramatic tension and dramatic poetry . . .' (p. 9). Stoll, in any case, is applying his understanding of Elizabethan dramatic technique and stage conventions to the problems generated by Othello's apparent reversal of character in the middle of the play and to the psychological improbability of the basic narrative line: Iago's misleading Othello. Most of the criticism which Professor Gardner surveys is at least implicitly concerned with these problems, and in the same number of *Shakespeare Survey* Ned B. Allen goes so far as to argue that 'Shakespeare wrote the two parts of *Othello* at different times – in different frames of mind – and . . . joined them carelessly' ('The Two Parts of "Othello"', p. 17).

² Brents Stirling, *Unity in Shakespearean Tragedy* (Columbia University Press, 1956), without reference to Renaissance formulations of the idea of honour, sees something like the same structure in the play. '. . . A psychological theme has been dominant from the start of the play. This theme, reputation, has appeared in its two aspects of normal regard for good name and egoistic, defensive concern for "face". Iago has embodied the latter side of the theme, and his morbid view of reputation is the one which finally possesses Othello in III.iii' (pp. 121–2). He is to a degree following G. R. Elliott, who in *Flaming Minister* (Durham, N. C., 1953) sees Othello as being possessed of both 'right self-esteem' and 'wrong pride'. Regarding the structure of the play, Stirling notes, 'Mr Elliott points to a "coalescing" of the Iago and Othello roles in III.iii (*Flaming Minister*, p. 126, 137). But he predicates this on a previously developed shallowness of Othello's self-centered love' (p. 122, n. 6). Reference to common Renaissance ideas about honour, rather than to the 'psychological theme' of reputation, demonstrates that this structure is deliberate and pervasive.

³ Watson remarks that 'revenge for adultery, by the murder of both wife and adulterer, was tolerated in the early laws of every European country' (p. 160). This is probably an excessive judgment, but the fact that honour required revenge, whatever the law might be, is clear. Fredson Bowers, *Elizabethan Revenge Tragedy, 1587–1642* (Princeton, 1940), compares the temperate English with the more severe Italian views on the matter, and quotes Fynes Moryson, *Shakespeare's Europe*, ed. Charles Hughes (London, 1903), as evidence of the severity to English eyes of the Italian attitude. 'Adulteries (as all furyes of Jelousy, or signs of making love, to wives, daughters and sisters) are commonly [by the Italians] prosecuted by priuate reuenge, and by murther . . .' (p. 50). Romei has Gualinguo begin his list of reasons that a woman guilty of unchaste behaviour is 'of harder condition' than a man by stating that 'if she be married, with her owne, shee also staineth the honour of her husband' (*The Courtiers Academie*, p. 97). Most Renaissance drama which deals at all with the matter reflects this common attitude. John W. Draper, 'Honest Iago', *Publications of the Modern Language Asso-*

ciation, XLVI (1931), cites *Rule a Wife*, *Philaster*, *English Traveller*, and *The Maid's Tragedy* as instances in which 'revenge for infidelity was regarded ... as a sort of justice'. His suggestion is that Iago is also 'in some sense justified in revenging the supposed infidelity of Emilia' (p. 730).

⁴ Giraldi Cinthio, from *Hecatommithi*, tr. L. F. Dean and Joseph B. Cary, *A Casebook on Othello*, ed. L. F. Dean (New York, 1961), pp. 263–4.

⁵ Ashley, p. 57.

⁶ Cinthio, p. 257.

⁷ Craig, pp. 958–9, n. to ll. 205–7.

⁸ 'The Two Parts of "Othello"', p. 17.

⁹ '"Othello": A retrospect', p. 5.

Chapter 7

KING LEAR
The Wages of Virtue

In *King Lear* common Renaissance assumptions about honour serve
to identify the nature of Lear's early delusions, his anguish, and his
moral regeneration. The idea Shakespeare initially gives Lear of the
sort of thing honour is and of the validity of its demands is but one of
the delusions which the play strips from Lear, but all of his early
expectations are touched by his concern for the honour he thinks,
quite conventionally, that his various roles justly demand. Lear's
expectations of love from Cordelia, obedience from Kent, and gratitude
from Goneril and Regan are made perverse by the play, but they are for
Lear absolute, precisely because he considers those qualities to be
inevitable manifestations of nature's universal laws. So, no doubt, did
a good many of the members of Shakespeare's audiences. If this King
is somehow perverting these values, the audience's first reactions might
well have been, it is not the values themselves, but Lear who is suspect.
Old men generally, fathers especially, and kings most particularly of
all have very clearly defined roles, and if they play those roles well the
real and various forms of honour, as always, are among their chief
rewards. Hooker, the voice of orthodoxy, had described the duty men
have to honour other men, particularly their parents and their kings,[1]
and it is clear that, were Lear calling for honour and obedience and love
in appropriate ways, every right-thinking member of Shakespeare's
first audiences would automatically have assumed his right to claim
them.

Shakespeare, however, develops his protagonist's tragedy in a
manner which subjects these orthodox values themselves to a most
sceptical scrutiny. Lear, at the outset rigorously convinced that honour,
love, and obedience as they display themselves in human behaviour are
inevitable and valid because they are manifestations of nature, is

136

stripped of his delusions so that he, and we, may observe directly the nature which even such apparently benign forms of human conduct can pervert.[2] ''Tis worse than murther,/ To do upon respect such violent outrage' (II. iv. 22–3), Lear says to Kent in the stocks, but the experience on the heath moves Lear to an understanding of nature and of man's place in it which makes his earlier concern for 'respect' and all the other conventionalized forms of human behaviour petty by comparison. *King Lear* is, as has often been remarked, thus like *Hamlet* in being more explicitly philosophical than the other great tragedies. Ideas of honour are part of that philosophical concern, but unlike *Julius Caesar* or *Othello* the tragedy in *King Lear* does not spring from the dilemma implicit in perfect obedience to such seemingly valid demands as those of honour. Lear sees honour for what it can become, just as he sees conventional forms of obedience, justice, and love for what they can become, and is consequently brought to a more positive knowledge of the tragic world he inhabits.

A pattern of ideas strikingly similar to that in *King Lear* informs Fulke Greville's *Alaham*, and though the scenes of the play are developed with Greville's customary and intriguing obscurity, reference to its Choruses, which draw with broad strokes many of the same judgments of honour and other 'human forts' that Shakespeare dramatizes, provides a sort of ethical blueprint of the more complex world of *King Lear*. The Second Chorus of Alaham is set as an argument among Furies, i.e. Malice, Craft, Pride, Corrupt Reason, and Evil Spirits, who are debating with considerable puzzlement why Caine, Hala, and Alaham in particular, but mankind in general, have not succumbed to the evil plans the Furies have prepared. The entire debate is a sort of mad Ciceronian dialogue to which each Furie contributes by claiming that his particular form of evil is the most effective cause of man's depravity. 'Wherein doe we fayle?' Malice asks, and thereby precipitates his quarrel with Craft, who responds: 'In that we mankind vnto fame entayle'. But Malice is content with the pernicious influences of fame, for 'That breakes Religions bounds, and makes him ours,/ By forming his God out of his owne powers'.[3] Greville, in the *Inquisition upon Fame and Honour*, had argued for the practical usefulness of man's capacity to create a god out of honour in this decadent world; here he has Craft, appropriately, argue that fame ill-serves their evil purposes, for 'fame keepes outward order, and supports./ For shame and honour are strong humane forts' (15–16). Pride, the next stage of the hierarchy, enters the argument to claim superiority over Craft on the ground that he can control everything 'with honors name'.

> For while you feare your true tormentor, *shame*,
> I swallow all at once, with honors name.
>
> (57–8)

Corrupt Reason, describing the other contenders as 'base *Subalterns*', claims to be lord of the Furies and thus to work the most devastating evil on man.

> I breake the banks of dutie, honor, faith;
> And subiect am to no power, but to death. . . .
> Wrong I attire in purple robes of might,
> That State may helpe it to be infinite.
> And who is fitter here to rule you all,
> Than I, that gaue you being, by my fall?
>
> (67–8, 79–82)

These are, thus far, easily recognizable allegorical figures, and Greville is, thus far, merely orthodox in assigning 'corrupt reason' the chief place in this hierarchy of evil. The limitation to which he has Corrupt Reason admit is also orthodox; vice has no positive power, but depends on man's defects.

> Know therefore all you shadow-louing Spirits!
> Who haue no being, but in mans demerits,
> That infinite desires, and finite power,
> At once, can neuer all mankinde deuoure.
> Though men be all ours, and all we but one;
> The vice yet cannot build, or stand alone.
>
> (83–8)

At this point Greville leaves his heretofore orthodox description of the sources of evil and introduces the chief element in his hierarchy, the nearly Manichean 'Euill Spirits'.[4] They represent a positive power which vice is able to execute because the age is decadent. It is this emphasis on the general decadence of mankind, which reflects itself in the particular decadence of various standards of behaviour, which brings us close to the pattern of similar ideas in *King Lear*. Because of the times, the Evil Spirits argue, 'wrong needs no veile', and they list as instances of the unnecessary veils the Furies have intruded a variety of seemingly virtuous standards of behaviour which now mask the evil which man is actually prepared to accept openly. The 'veils' allow hypocrisy, and thus provide, from the Evil Spirits' point of view, an unnecessary show of virtue.

> *Lusts open face* this Age will easily beare,
> And hope here currant is to all, but feare.
> Wrong needs no veile, where times doe tyrannize;
> And what, but lacke of heart, is then vnwise;
> Age hath descri'd those toyes to be but name,
> Which in the worlds youth did beare reall fame;
> *Iustice, Religion, Honour, Humblenesse*;
> *Shaddowes*, which not well mixt, make beauty lesse.
> They helpe to smother, not inlarge our fire,
> By putting painted maskes on mans desire. ....
>
> (111–20)

The Furies, thus, '*Circe*-like, change men to beasts,/ Which beasts turne men againe' (123–4). The 'painted maskes' which allow these 'beasts' to 'turne men againe' are assailable, however, and the Evil Spirits know there is a 'Tempter fitted' for each of the various roles which men might play.

> A *feare* in Great men still, to lose their might;
> And in the meane, *ambition* infinite;
> *Truth*, in the witty held but as a notion;
> *Honor*, the Old mans God; the Youth's promotion.
> All which opposing powers, yet doe agree
> To worke corruption in humanity.
>
> (135–40)[5]

Goneril, Regan, Cornwall, Oswald, and Edmund are beasts not 'turne[d] men againe', and for them 'wrong needs no veile'.[6] Lear comes to comprehend that this is so, and also to realize that the forms of honour, love, and obedience which he had thought so justly his, make him participate, however unwittingly, in that malignant world. Honour, like the other values Greville's chorus lists, becomes a veil for evil in both *Alaham* and *King Lear* when it becomes self-contained. In the opening scene Kent knows that honour is rightfully bound to virtue, so he performs his role as adviser perfectly by defending Cordelia even in the face of Lear's wrath.

> Think'st thou that duty shall have dread to speak
> When power to flattery bows? To plainness honour's bound
> When majesty falls to folly.
>
> (I. i. 147–9)[7]

But honour is, for Lear, 'the old man's God', and Shakespeare leaves no doubt that it is the formal affront to that honour, rather than whatever substance may be in Kent's advice, which angers Lear. He has vowed to abandon Cordelia, and his response to Kent's efforts shows exactly how formal codes divorce themselves from the human behaviour they presumably regulate to become ends in themselves.

> Hear me recreant!
> On thine allegiance, hear me!
> Since thou hast sought to make us break our vow –
> Which we durst never yet – and with strain'd pride
> To come between our sentence and our power, –
> Which nor our nature nor our place can bear, –
> Our potency make good, take thy reward.
>
> (I. i. 166–72)

This exchange expresses in terms of honour the dichotomy between substantive values and their formal manifestation which is the chief thematic concern of the first two scenes. The narrative, of course, demands that Lear reject his good daughter and be deluded by his evil ones, but Shakespeare develops this basic narrative scheme by emphasizing Lear's certainty that the formal modes of behaviour he demands are valid because they manifest nature's laws. Cordelia, because she does not provide the formal, if excessive, declaration of love which Lear thinks justly his, is 'a wretch whom nature is asham'd/ Almost t'acknowledge hers' (I. i. 212–13). Lear justifies dividing his kingdom by assuming that the political order he thus establishes will prevent 'future strife' (I. i. 43). Lear hands over to Cornwall and Albany his 'power,/ Preeminence, and all the large effects/ That troop with majesty', but retains his hundred knights and 'the name, and all th' additions to a king' (I. i. 129–31, 135). The wrong that Lear does is thus veiled, much as Greville's Second Chorus works out the idea, by his assurance that his actions are in accord with perfectly valid forms of behaviour. And, again as in Greville's chorus, it is not merely that the King is mistaken; the values themselves, which, as the Evil Spirits have

it, 'in the worlds youth did beare reall fame', are perverted. Kent and
Cordelia and France stand in the scene as assurance that those values
can be validly expressed in human behaviour, but it is for them, as for
Goneril and Regan, the expository, not the concluding act. Shakespeare
has set rival forces in motion, and the battleground is the soul of a king
whose moral vision is impaired because he believes that the forms of
honour, love, and duty which he requires reflect absolute and natural
values.

The next scene establishes Gloucester's dilemma in precisely the
same terms. It is, as with Lear, a requirement of the narrative that
Gloucester be tricked by his evil son into rejecting his good one, and
Shakespeare again develops the narrative scheme by assigning to
Gloucester the same sort of commitment to the conventional forms of
virtue which so afflicts Lear. Parallels with the ethical plan of *Alaham*
continue, too, for each 'Tempter fitted' for man's various estates is
present in the scene. Mean in fortune, Edmund has '*ambition* infinite'.
Witty, he holds '*Truth* . . . but as a notion'.

> A credulous father! and a brother noble,
> Whose nature is so far from doing harms
> That he suspects none; on whose foolish honesty
> My practices ride easy! I see the business.
> Let me, if not by birth, have lands by wit;
> All with me's meet that I can fashion fit.

(I. II. 168–73)

Young and – more tellingly – illegitimate, '*Honour*' is Edmund's
promotion.

> Wherefore should I
> Stand in the plaguè of custom, and perm t
> The curiosity of nations to deprive me,
> For that I am some twelve or fourteen moon-shines
> Lag of a brother? Why bastard? wherefore base?
> When my dimensions are as well compact,
> My mind as generous, and my shape as true,
> As honest madam's issue? Why brand they us
> With base? with baseness? bastardy? base, base?
> Who, in the lusty stealth of nature, take
> More composition and fierce quality

к

> Than doth, within a dull, stale, tired bed,
> Go to th' creating a whole tribe of fops
> Got 'tween asleep and wake?
>
> (I. II. 2-15)

These are all but one of the 'opposing powers' which 'doe agree/ To worke corruption in humanity'. The missing power, the *'feare* in Great men still, to lose their might' is supplied by Gloucester's response to Edgar's supposed letter. Gloucester's delusion is a given of the narrative; the important contribution the scene makes to the structure of the play is that the intricate thematic connections between the two plots is begun here by Shakespeare's developing a similar context in which the delusion of the two old men operates. The scene dramatizes Gloucester's delusion by making the letter and the other insinuations which Edmund produces question the formal filial relationships which Gloucester thinks unimpeachable.

> 'This policy and reverence of age makes the world bitter to the best of our times; keeps our fortunes from us till our oldness cannot relish them. I begin to find an idle and fond bondage in the oppression of aged tyranny, who sways, not as it hath power, but as it is suffer'd.'
>
> (I. II. 45-50)

The passions this letter arouses are, of course, anguished and personal. 'My son Edgar!' Gloucester responds, 'Had he a hand to write this? A heart and brain to breed it in?' (I. II. 55-6). But the emphasis of the scene is on Gloucester's unquestioning assurance that the formal conventions which regulate the relationship between father and son are laws of nature. When Edmund insinuates that Edgar believes that 'sons at perfect age, and fathers declining, the father should be as ward to the son, and the son manage his revenue' (I. II. 69-71), Shakespeare has Gloucester see Edgar as an 'unnatural, detested, brutish villain' (I. II. 74). Edgar's supposed affront has, in Gloucester's eyes, made him guilty of the same sort of crime against nature which caused Lear to see Cordelia as 'a wretch whom nature is asham'd/ Almost t'acknowledge hers'. Both Gloucester and Lear are thus introduced as being incapable of questioning the validity of such conventions as the honour, obedience, and love they think due to them. Even keeping Lear's example constantly before himself – and the audience – Gloucester can only find an explanation for the present disorder in 'These late eclipses in the sun and moon' (I. II. 98).

Lear's belief in the conventional forms of human behaviour is deep-seated, but in the remainder of Act I and in Act II Shakespeare subjects it to some severe shocks. The role honour has in the play is most apparent here, for it is largely in terms of honour that Shakespeare develops Goneril's and Regan's various affronts to Lear. The hundred knights are a convenient symbol of the honour Lear thinks due to him, and as Goneril and Regan chip away at those knights the foundations of Lear's world crumble.[8] The knight who follows the suddenly insolent Oswald out is the harbinger of Lear's trials.

> ... To my judgment, your Highness is not entertain'd with that ceremonious affection as you were wont.
>
> (I. IV. 54-5)

Goneril's confrontation with Lear brings the matter to a head. Goneril enters to warn Lear that if he does not, she shall correct his 'insolent retinue', a correction which in a 'wholesome weal' would 'shame' him. This might to an unwary modern reader appear but the minor beginnings of Goneril's plot; to the Lear whom I. I. had defined as having an unshakable expectation of the forms of honour due to him it is incomprehensible. 'Are you our daughter?' Lear asks. 'Doth any here know me?/ ... Who is it that can tell me who I am?' (I. IV. 206, 214, 218). Lear's conception of his world as a place where honour is inevitably paid where it is due is being challenged, and when Goneril condemns the knights as 'disorder'd ... debosh'd, and bold', and asserts that the 'shame itself doth speak/ For instant remedy' (I. IV. 230, 234-5), Lear responds to the affront to his retinue's, and thus to his own, honour violently, but typically. Only a 'degenerate bastard' is capable of this affront, for no child of his could devise it; Lear's followers are 'men of choice and rarest parts,/ That all particulars of duty know,/ And in the most exact regard support/ The worships of their name' (I. IV. 252-7). Lear now sees Cordelia's as 'a most small fault', but he is still judging Goneril's action by the same standards which had led him to banish Cordelia, for Shakespeare has him still convinced that the nature he calls on to curse Goneril validates the forms of behaviour which he demands. The 'wretch whom nature is asham'd/ Almost t'acknowledge hers' is, in Lear's eyes, the same as the daughter Lear now sees Goneril to be, and for the same reasons. As Cordelia there failed to provide the

143

formal declaration of love which Lear believes nature to demand, so
Goneril has here maligned the honour which Lear assumes to be justly
his.

The other shock with which Shakespeare confronts Lear's beliefs in
this scene is also developed in terms of honour. When Lear returns
from discovering that Goneril has taken away fifty of his followers 'at
a clap', he has to struggle to resist breaking down into unmanly tears.

> Life and death! I am asham'd
> That thou hast power to shake my manhood thus;
> That these hot tears, which break from me perforce,
> Should make thee worth them.
>
> (I. iv. 285–8)[9]

The scene has thus developed the beginnings of Lear's trial as a series
of increasingly grievous affronts to his honour, to which Lear responds
with increasing outrage. When we see him at Gloucester's castle, in
hopeful pursuit of Regan, another and more grievous shock to his
honour greets him.

Shakespeare makes Lear, in spite of Kent in the stocks and of Kent's
assurances that Lear's son-in-law and daughter put him there, unable to
conceive that they could do his honour such disservice. Typically, he
considers the dishonour worse than murder.

> They durst not do't;
> They would not, could not do't. 'Tis worse than murder
> To do upon respect such violent outrage.
>
> (II. iv. 21–3)

And, typically, he tries to persuade himself that this disservice results
from some illness of the Duke's, for he cannot believe that unimpaired
nature could permit such an affront to honour and duty.

> The King would speak with Cornwall; the dear father
> Would with his daughter speak, commands her service.
> Are they inform'd of this? My breath and blood!
> Fiery? the fiery Duke? tell the hot Duke that –
> No, but not yet! May be he is not well.
> Infirmity doth still neglect all office
> Whereto our health is bound. We are not ourselves
> When nature, being oppress'd, commands the mind
> To suffer with the body.
>
> (II. iv. 97–105)

But Kent is still in the stocks, and, turning to him, Lear realizes that he cannot blame infirmity for this to him otherwise inexplicable flaw in nature which has permitted such dishonour.

> Death on my state! Wherefore
> Should he sit here? This act persuades me
> That this remotion of the Duke and her
> Is practice only.
>
> (II. IV. 108–11)

When Cornwall and Regan enter, Shakespeare dramatizes Lear's conviction that nature validates his expectation of honour by using precisely the same terms he had employed in the earlier scene with Goneril. If Regan is not prepared to give Lear the honourable welcome he believes the filial relationship to demand, she cannot in Lear's eyes be his daughter.

> *Reg.* I am glad to see your Highness.
> *Lear.* Regan, I think you are; I know what reason
> I have to think so. If thou shouldst not be glad,
> I would divorce me from thy mother's tomb,
> Sepulchring an adultress.
>
> (II. IV. 124–8)

And, he assures Regan, she will never have his curse, for she obeys nature's demands.

> 'Tis not in thee
> To grudge my pleasures, to cut off my train,
> To bandy hasty words, to scant my sizes,
> And, in conclusion, to oppose the bolt
> Against my coming in. Thou better know'st
> The offices of nature, bond of childhood,
> Effects of courtesy, dues of gratitude.
>
> (II. IV. 170–6)

But Regan refuses to provide him welcome, and when Goneril enters they begin to whittle away at the remaining knights. Lear still cannot conceive that it is possible, within the order of nature, for them to treat him so, so he must explain Goneril, as he had earlier tried to explain Cornwall's behaviour, as a disease in nature.

> But yet thou art my flesh, my blood, my daughter;
> Or rather a disease that's in my flesh,
> Which I must needs call mine. Thou art a boil,
> A plague sore, or embossed carbuncle
> In my corrupted blood.

(II. IV. 218–22)

Yet having seen Goneril as a disease in nature, and having called down his horrible curse on her, when Regan deprives him of half of his remaining knights, Lear pathetically turns back to Goneril. Committed to his demand for formal and external expressions of love and honour, Lear is reduced to a pathetic because merely numerical evaluation of that love and honour, the logical conclusion of the standards which caused him to reject Cordelia.

> Those wicked creatures yet do look well-favour'd
> When others are more wicked; not being the worst
> Stands in some rank of praise. [To Goneril] I'll go with thee.
> Thy fifty yet doth double five-and-twenty,
> And thou art twice her love.

(II. IV. 253–7)

When all the knights are removed by Regan's 'What need one?' Lear's dishonour is complete. The speech with which Shakespeare has Lear respond to this ultimate affront is affecting, for Lear even in the midst of affliction is kept heroic, but it is not, as has often been suggested, the beginnings of a new moral awareness in Lear.[10] It is, rather, the final statement of the Lear defined for us by the first scene, a Lear who continues to believe that the forms which convention has created, here still symbolized by the honourable retinue he thinks due to him, are valid manifestations of nature's laws. His 'reason not the need' is his last appeal for his knights, and Shakespeare has Lear argue only for such formal and external accommodations as they represent. 'Our basest beggars/ Are in the poorest thing superfluous'. Lear begins. 'Allow not nature more than nature needs,/ Man's life is cheap as beast's' (II. IV. 261–4). What Lear explicitly means by 'need', clearly, is the form of honour represented by his hundred knights. Shakespeare here gives Lear the same concern for form, as firmly if more poignantly expressed, which had led him to dismiss Cordelia. For Lear to remark that the basest beggar is in the poorest 'thing' superfluous calls attention to his continued concern for the external and formal marks of humanity, and Shakespeare has him continue by arguing that the same principle which permits his daughters elaborate dress permits his honourable retinue. 'If only to go warm were gorgeous', Lear asserts, 'Why, nature needs not what thou gorgeous wear'st,/ Which scarcely keeps thee warm. But, for true need –' Lear here breaks off the futile argument to call for 'patience, patience I need' (II. IV. 266–8), but the rhetoric of the sentence makes clear the meaning. 'If' only the practical function of clothing were the issue, nature would not require the elaborate dress of his daughters. 'But' there is a true need beyond that required for mere existence, and it is clearly of a piece with the need for conventional forms such as honour which Lear has been expressing since the first scene of the play. Similarly, the patience which Lear calls for when he breaks off his argument is the patience which will allow him to regain his erstwhile position, the position towards which all the formal expressions of love, duty, and honour flowed. 'Touch me with noble anger', he begs the gods, 'and let not women's weapons, water-drops,/ Stain my man's cheeks!' (II. IV. 273–5). His daughters are 'unnatural hags', and he swears to revenge himself by destroying them, the only action which could vindicate the beliefs he has held since the beginning of the play.

> I will have such revenges on you both
> That all the world shall – I will do such things –
> What they are yet, I know not; but they shall be
> The terrors of the earth!
>
> (II. IV. 276–9)

This is the same Lear that rejected Cordelia, but it is the last time we hear from him. His experience on the heath will fashion in him a new understanding of nature and of man's part in it.

The state to which Lear is reduced in Act III is an elemental one. Again, reference to the ideas expressed in Greville's *Alaham* can help explain the ethical framework of the action in *King Lear*. The Third Chorus of that play, a dialogue between 'Good, and Euill Spirits', debates the relative power of good and evil in the world and examines the origins of evil. The Evil Spirits describe the innocent state of the world in 'the infancy of time' in terms remarkably similar to those Shakespeare uses to describe Lear's experience on the heath, for they argue that, because of man's ambitious desire for the outward forms of honour and glory, this innocence was self-defeating.

Besides, *Mappe* clearly out your [the Good Spirits] infinite extent,
Euen in the infancy of time, when much was innocent,
Could this world then yeeld ought to enuie, or desire,
Where pride of courage made men fall, and basenesse rais'd them
   higher?
Where they that would be great, to be so, must be least?
And where to beare, and suffer wrong, was vertues natiue crest?
Mans skinne, was then his silke; the worlds wild fruit, his food;
His wisdome, poore simplicity; his Trophies inward good.
No Maiesty, for power; nor glories, for mans worth;
Nor any end, but (as the plants) to bring each other forth.
Temples, and vessells fit for outward sacrifice,
As they came in, so go they out, with that which you count Vice.
The *Priesthood* few, and poore; No Throne, but open ayre:
For that which you call good, allowes of nothing that is faire.
No *Pyramis* rais'd vp aboue the force of Thunder,
Nor *Babel*-walles by *Greatnesse* built, for *Littlenesse* a wonder.
No Conquest testifying wit, with courage mixt;
As wheeles whereon the world must runne, and neuer can be fixt.
No Arts, or Characters to read the great God in;
Nor stories of acts done; for *these all entred with the sinne.*
A lasy calme, wherein each foole a pilot is:
The glory of the skilfull shines, where men may go amisse. ...
Then cease to blast the earth with your abstracted dreames
And striue no more to carry men against affections streames.
Nay rather tempt, and proue, if long life make them wise,
That must, to haue their beauties seeme, put out all fleshly eyes.

(19–46)

When Act III of *King Lear* opens, Lear, having seen perverted what he considered to be the 'natural' relationships between father and daughter, king and subject, and age and youth, calls on nature to reassert herself. His misanthropy is complete.

      And thou, all-shaking thunder,
Strike flat the thick rotundity o' th' world,
Crack Nature's moulds, all germains spill at once,
That make ingrateful man!

(III. II. 6–9)

But he is given a sense of the justice inherent in natural order, a sense which he has not exhibited before.

> Let the great gods,
> That keep this dreadful pudder o'er our heads,
> Find out their enemies now. Tremble, thou wretch,
> That hast within thee undivulged crimes,
> Unwhipp'd of justice. Hide thee, thou bloody hand;
> Thou perjur'd, and thou simular man of virtue
> That art incestuous. Caitiff, in pieces shake
> That under covert and convenient seeming
> Hast practis'd on man's life. Close pent-up guilts,
> Rive your concealing continents, and cry
> These dreadful summoners grace. I am a man
> More sinn'd against than sinning.
>
> (III. ii. 49–60)

This recognition on his part represents a significant change in a character who has heretofore concerned himself only with preserving 'The name, and all the additions to a king', for he here for the first time distinguishes between the substance of virtuous behaviour and the forms which he earlier believed inevitably to accompany that behaviour. When Lear encounters the unaccommodated man, stripped of all the 'Trophies', 'Maiesty', and 'glories' that Greville's Evil Spirits describe as having 'entred with the sinne', his recognition grows. Labouring under his commitment to the forms of honour, he had said of an affront to that honour:

> 'Tis worse than murder
> To do upon respect such violent outrage.
>
> (II. iv. 22–3)

But in Act III, he ignores the question of honour to consider the basic confrontation between unaccommodated man and elemental nature which Edgar's plight represents to him.

Thou wert better in thy grave than to answer with thy uncover'd body this extremity of the skies. Is man no more than this? Consider him well. Thou ow'st the worm no silk, the beast no hide, the sheep no wool, the cat no perfume. Ha! Here's three on's are sophisticated!

Thou art the thing itself; unaccommodated man is no more but such a poor, bare, forked animal as thou art. Off, off, you lendings!

(III. IV. 95–102)[11]

The unaccommodated man becomes, to Lear's madness, a 'learned Theban', a 'Noble philosopher', and an 'Athenian'. When this madness is viewed with reference to Lear's earlier 'sanity' it becomes apparent that his 'mad' concern with problems more elemental than the forms of honour and duty that he thought parents and kings to deserve marks the important difference. The trial that Lear assembles to examine Goneril and Regan is 'mad', but seems so precisely because he is no longer so convinced of the 'naturalness' of the outward order that honour and duty should create that he must consider his daughters 'a disease/ ... a boil/ ... an embossed carbuncle,/ In [his] corrupted blood' in order to explain their behaviour. Rather, he inquires into the basic cause of their action.

Then let them anatomize Regan. See what breeds about her heart. Is there any cause in nature that makes these hard hearts?

(III. VI. 73–5)

All Lear's fixed assumptions about his world have been stripped away, and nothing has as yet replaced them. His 'madness' is produced by this moral vacuum, and in the two central acts of the play Lear rails at the perversion of natural virtues which such forms as 'majesty' and 'glory' can produce. Though the 'beasts' have apparently 'turned men again', the forms which allow them to do so are damaging. The respect paid kings, Lear sees in an absolute reversal of his earlier conviction, is at odds with elemental nature.

When the rain came to wet me once,
and the wind to make me chatter; when the thunder would not peace at my bidding; there I found 'em, there I smelt 'em out. Go to, they are not men o' their words! They told me I was everything. 'Tis a lie – I am not ague-proof.

(IV. VI. 100–5)

Sexual chastity, and the concomitant idea that there is a natural bond between legitimate children and their parents has no justification in nature.

I pardon that man's life. What was thy cause?
Adultery?
Thou shalt not die. Die for adultery? No.
The wren goes to't, and the small gilded fly
Does lecher in my sight.
Let copulation thrive; for Gloucester's bastard son
Was kinder to his father than my daughters
Got 'tween the lawful sheets.

(IV. VI. 109–16)

Authority is a mere convention, and justice and guilt interchangeable masks.

> *Lear.* What, art mad? A man may see how this world goes with no
> eyes. Look with thine ears. See how yond justice rails upon yond
> simple thief. Hark in thine ear. Change places and, handy-dandy,
> which is the justice, which is the thief? Thou hast seen a farmer's
> dog bark at a beggar?
> *Glou.* Ay, sir.
> *Lear.* And the creature run from the cur? There thou mightst
> behold the great image of authority: a dog's obey'd in office.
> Thou rascal beadle, hold thy bloody hand!
> Why dost thou lash that whore? Strip thine own back.
> Thou hotly lust'st to use her in that kind
> For which thou whip'st her.

(IV. VI. 149–62)

Most particularly, the façades which honour and wealth can erect can absolutely invert right and wrong.

> *Lear.* Through tatter'd clothes small vices do appear;
> Robes and furr'd gowns hide all. Plate sin with gold,
> And the strong lance of justice hurtless breaks;
> Arm it in rags, a pygmy's straw does pierce it.

(IV. VI. 163–6)

What is notable in all this, however, is that Shakespeare has Lear continuously assume that absolute standards of right and wrong do exist, even though they do not display themselves in human behaviour. Misanthropy and despair cause Lear to preach to Gloucester:

When we are born, we cry that we are come
To this great stage of fools.

(IV. VI. 181–2)

But Lear, even here, is no cynic. Troilus thinks and persuades Hector
that nothing 'is aught, but as 'tis valu'd', and that play remains merely
cynical. But Shakespeare develops Lear's tragedy, in part, by keeping
him aware, in the central portion of the play, of the real values which
have so far escaped him – and mankind. The pernicious thing about
the various forms to which Lear has been committed is that they
become independent of the values they are ideally designed to protect.
By requiring the various forms of honour he thought due him, Lear
made the service, once again, greater than the god.

Gloucester's development in these two acts gives added scope to the
moral regeneration with which the play is concerned; Gloucester is
put in circumstances similar to those of the King, but by giving
Gloucester a different response to these circumstances, Shakespeare
allows himself to display the consequences of another reaction to the
play's central dilemmas. Men 'must', Greville's Evil Spirits say, 'to
haue their beauties seeme, put out all fleshly eyes'. When Gloucester's
'fleshly eyes' are put out, he is disabused of the mistake which Edmund's cunning and his own moral predisposition had produced. In
the moment before understanding comes, his persistence in his error
demonstrates that he continues to make the same facile assumptions
about the 'natural' relationship between parent and child that Lear has
made. He calls for revenge, the most pernicious demand that Shakespeare has the decadent forms of honour make, assuming that nature
requires it.

All dark and comfortless! Where's my son Edmund?
Edmund, enkindle all the sparks of nature
To quit this horrid act.

(III. VII. 84–6)

Told the truth, his 'fleshly eyes' are allegorically as well as literally put
out, and his 'beauties seeme'.

O my follies! Then Edgar was abus'd.
Kind gods, forgive me that, and prosper him!

(III. VII. 90–1)

The despair into which he is consequently introduced is more thorough than Lear's; the belief in an ultimate and valid moral standard which permits Lear's condemnation of the standards of this world is lacking in Gloucester. The bases of thought and action which he had accepted for himself having been stripped away, Gloucester sees men as valueless creatures in the hands of indifferent or malignant deities.

> As flies to wanton boys, are we to th' gods.
> They kill us for their sport.
>
> (IV. i. 36–7)

His attempt to kill himself, the ultimate expression of despair, fails, but even after his 'rebirth', Gloucester's despair is more destructive than Lear's. We see Gloucester faced with only two more decisions. In the first, having but recently determined to 'bear/ Affliction till it do cry out itself/ "Enough, enough," and die' (IV. vi. 75–7), Gloucester responds to Oswald's intent to murder him:

> Now let thy friendly hand
> Put strength enough to't.
>
> (IV. vi. 229–30)

In the second, being implored by Edgar to flee the victorious forces of Goneril and Regan, Gloucester refuses:

> No further, sir. A man may rot even here.
>
> (V. ii. 8)

In both cases, of course, Edgar prevents the consequences of Gloucester's despair, as he had earlier prevented his suicide, but it is notable that no such despair seizes Lear. Though he makes him mad, Shakespeare gives Lear the greater moral stature by having him continue to rail against the 'Robes and furr'd gowns' which can invert virtue and vice and thereby pervert natural order. A bit of onstage action, which has no other apparent purpose, emphasizes this difference in stature. Thirty-five lines or so before Gloucester urges Oswald's 'friendly hand' to be strong enough to kill him, Shakespeare puts Lear in what the King also considers to be mortal danger.

> I will die bravely, like a smug bridegroom. What!
> I will be jovial. Come, come, I am a king;
> My masters, know you that?
>
> (IV. vi. 197–9)

And though on the modern stage Lear's response to the danger he sees is often played as a sort of sly but childish game, a consequence of his madness, certainly Lear's next lines are intended as a positive contrast to Gloucester's merely negative despair.

> *Gent.* You are a royal one, and we obey you.
> *Lear.* Then there's life in't. Come, an you get it, you shall get it by running. Sa, sa, sa, sa!
>
> (IV. VI. 200–2)

When we next see Lear, Shakespeare presents him as seeing clearly, though haltingly, that he is entering a different world than the elemental and purgative one of the heath.

> You do me wrong to take me out o' th' grave.
> Thou art a soul in bliss; but I am bound
> Upon a wheel of fire, that mine own tears
> Do scald like molten lead.
>
> (IV. VII. 45–8)

To understand the new perspective from which Lear views his world, and the connection between this perspective and Lear's earlier and destructive commitment to the various conventional forms of love and duty and honour, it is useful to turn again to the Third Chorus of Greville's *Alaham*. The Evil Spirits, it will be recalled, had argued that good is doomed, for to be appealing to human beings it depends on those aspects – fame, honour, etc. – which can destroy it. They conclude:

> Besides; take from the world that which you reckon *Sinne*;
> And she must be, as at the first, for euer to beginne.
> A glorious, spacious wombe fram'd to containe but one;
> Since he, that in it will be yours, is sure to be alone.
> Keepe therefore where you are; descend not, but ascend:
> For, *vnderneath the Sun, be sure no braue State is your friend.*
>
> (65–70)

The response which the Good Spirits make to this charge can reveal a great deal about the regenerate state Lear finds himself in in Act V. The Good Spirits first argue that evil's apparent success is misleading, for it is variable and impermanent.

What haue you wonne by this, but that curst vnder Sunne,
You make, and marre; throw downe, and raise; as euer to beginne?
... Not truth, but truth-like grounds is that you worke vpon,
Varying in all but this, *that you can neuer long be one.*

(71–6)

The cause of this impermanence is clear; if pernicious, such things as honour or reputation are, among other things, self-defeating. Consequently, their fulfilment is their destruction.

Let ill example in to staine the *Christian* Nation;
The same excesse destroyes at last, which first gaue reputation.

(93–4)

Though 'truth' is an 'easie foe', it, being substance, must persist where evil, lacking substance, must cease. The human being who emerges from this conflict, the Good Spirits further argue, is more than saved from the delusions of evil; his purgation has strengthened him.

If to be nothing be the best that could befall;
Your subtile *Orbes*, to reall beings, then must needs be thrall.
And so proue to the good but like those *showres of raine,*
Which, while they wet the husbandman, yet multiply his gaine.

(105–8)

This image describes the ubiquitous pattern of redemption, and Lear, as the concluding parts of the play define him, is strengthened in precisely this fashion. His first speeches and acts when he awakens demonstrate his humility, a humility which has been prepared for in Act IV by his recognition that he is not 'ague-proof', and a humility which, when compared with the 'honourable' demands Lear had made in Act I, is precisely defined by Greville's Good Spirits: '*The same excesse destroyes at last, which first gaue reputation*'. Shakespeare has Cordelia, in Act V, suggest a confrontation with the victorious Goneril and Regan, but Lear's response demonstrates how far he has come from his sometime compelling concern with 'the name, and all the additions to a king'.

No, no, no, no! Come, let's away to prison.
We two alone will sing like birds i' th' cage.
When thou dost ask me blessing, I'll kneel down,

And ask of thee forgiveness. So we'll live,
And pray, and sing, and tell old tales, and laugh
At gilded butterflies, and hear poor rogues
Talk of court news; and we'll talk with them too –
Who loses and who wins; who's in, who's out –
And take upon 's the mystery of things,
As if we were God's spies; and we'll wear out,
In a wall'd prison, packs and sects of great ones
That ebb and flow by th' moon.

(V. III. 8–19)

The 'packs and sects of great ones/ That ebb and flow by th' moon'
are very like the transitory Evil Spirits in *Alaham*, which the Good
Spirits condemn: 'Like *Meteors* in the ayre, you blaze but to burne out,/
And change your shapes ... to leaue weake eyes in doubt' (73–4).
Lear's disdain for these 'great ones' illustrates his regeneration; his view
of this sort of evil as self-defeating, which Shakespeare immediately
introduces, illustrates the positive moral strength which his regeneration has brought him.

Upon such sacrifices, my Cordelia,
The gods themselves throw incense. Have I caught thee?
He that parts us shall bring a brand from heaven
And fire us hence like foxes. Wipe thine eyes.
The goodyears shall devour them, flesh and fell,
Ere they shall make us weep! We'll see 'em starv'd first.

(V. III. 20–5)

Kenneth Muir, in the Arden edition of the play, citing the *OED*,
defines *goodyear* as a word that 'came to be used in imprecatory phrases,
as denoting some undefined malefic power or agency', and, disagreeing
with the various other interpretations he lists, conjectures that 'Lear
may mean that Goneril and Regan will be destroyed not by misfortunes
but by their evil prosperity, and till the day of their ruin he and
Cordelia will not deign to weep'.[12] The speech, so read, indicates that
Lear's experience has not merely purged him of his earlier, destructive
commitments, it has also taught him that the various perverted but
conventional forms of duty, fame, and honour that 'keep outward
order' will destroy themselves. He is thus given a positive moral understanding of a unique kind in the plays. The closest parallel to the sort

of understanding given Lear, and consequently the play which most closely approximates *King Lear*'s display of the nature perverted by these conventional forms of behaviour, is to be found in *Hamlet*. In both, the tragedy resides primarily in the inscrutable world figured forth by the play rather than in a grievous – or even 'tragic' – fault in the protagonist. The narrative turns on the errors in judgment which Shakespeare assigns Lear from the outset, but those errors do not provoke tragedy in the same way that Brutus' or Othello's errors do. During the course of the play Lear is wrenched away from his early commitment to the conventional forms of love and duty and honour and near the end of the play expresses a sense of universal and natural justice to which his early errors had blinded him. The moral insight, consequently, which Shakespeare develops in Lear is potentially incompatible with the play's tragic pattern. The play, after all, has in its various ways urged that there is something self-destructive in evil, as *Alaham*'s Good Spirits had insisted by saying that the Evil Spirits '*can neuer long be one*', and has brought its protagonist – and its audience – to see the perversions to which such conventional values as honour and duty are subject. Where, then, one might ask, lies the tragedy? If the 'goodyears shall devour them' is not *King Lear* rather a Divine comedy or, more accurately, a natural comedy than a tragedy?

As in *Hamlet*, Shakespeare provides the tragic structure of the play by developing Lear's moral awareness in a world nevertheless subject to outrageous fortune. For Hamlet, 'since no man knows aught of what he leaves', the 'readiness is all'. The Lear described by Kent's speech, 'If fortune brag of two she lov'd and hated,/ One of them we behold' (V. III. 280–1), rails against rather than accepts the world that can permit Cordelia's murder.

> Howl, howl, howl! O, you are men of stones.
> Had I your tongues and eyes, I'ld use them so
> That heaven's vault should crack.
>
> (V. III. 257–9)

His moral perceptions are distant, long-sighted ones, for the values that he sees do not inevitably exercise themselves in human affairs. The whole tragic pattern of the play is copied by a brief series of speeches in this concluding scene. Albany's speech regarding the new establishment of the kingdom is perfectly orthodox in the connection it draws between virtue and the honour due to virtue.

L   157

> [*To* Edgar *and* Kent] ... You, to your rights;
> With boot, and such addition as your honours
> Have more than merited. – All friends shall taste
> The wages of their virtue, and all foes
> The cup of their deservings.
>
> (V. III. 300–4)

Albany's talk of 'wages' and of the 'addition' which virtue merits is uncomfortably close to the attitude with which Lear began the play. His is, to be sure, a seemingly just rewarding of virtue, but we have learned that these 'rewards' are among the forms which so afflict human behaviour. Albany's speech represents an effort to re-establish the conventional forms that keep outward order. But Shakespeare immediately turns the audience's attention away from this effort to the basic tragic condition which the play has developed. 'O, see, see!' Albany cries, and we turn to Lear's unanswerable question.

> Why should a dog, a horse, a rat, have life,
> And thou no breath at all?
>
> (V. III. 306–7)

Shakespeare has given Lear a unique moral perception and, consequently, a unique stature among his tragic protagonists. Kent's epitaph articulates the tragic context which frames that perception and that stature.

> Vex not his ghost. O, let him pass! He hates him
> That would upon the rack of this tough world
> Stretch him out longer.
>
> (V. III. 313–15)

It is apparent that ideas of honour contribute in a different way to *King Lear* than they do to such earlier plays as *Othello* or *Julius Caesar*. There, man's service to honour is at the centre of the tragedy. In *King Lear*, honour is but one of the conventional ideas to which Shakespeare initially commits Lear. The various affronts to that honour and the anguish with which Lear responds to those affronts serve to demonstrate the thoroughness of Lear's delusion, but Lear's deluded commitment to honour does not precipitate his tragedy in the same way that Othello's, for instance, does. In the tragedies following *King Lear*, notably *Macbeth*,[13] *Antony and Cleopatra*, and *Coriolanus*, ideas of honour are also introduced largely as a means of delineating one aspect of the plays' conflicts. Duncan knows that he owes Macbeth honour for subduing the rebels, and Macbeth knows that he is abandoning the conventionally virtuous and honourable course to pursue his ambitious ends. 'We will proceed no further in this business', Macbeth tells his wife. '[Duncan] hath honour'd me of late, and I have bought/ Golden opinions from all sorts of people,/ Which would be worn now in their newest gloss,/ Not cast aside so soon' (I. VII. 31–5). Shakespeare develops Macbeth's ambition as the obverse of the virtuous pursuit of honour. Honour serves, in *Antony and Cleopatra*, to identify the Roman Antony who knows he must break 'these strong Egyptian fetters . . ./ Or lose [himself] in dotage' (I. II. 109–10). Coriolanus is as much the perfect man of honour as Hotspur was. Robert Ashley, wary, with all definers of true honour, of ambition, would no doubt have found Coriolanus' unwillingness to hear his 'nothings monster'd' the perfectly honourable response. 'He had rather venture all his limbs for honour,' Menenius remarks to the Tribunes, 'Than one on's ears to hear it' (II. II. 74, 77–8). Coriolanus' pure commitment to honour conflicts with pragmatic political demands and with the schemes of the Tribunes, but, as in *Macbeth* and *Antony and Cleopatra*, honour serves largely to define one aspect of the conflict. Like *1 Henry IV*, these plays are in part formed around the contest between honour and some other claim on men's behaviour. Each play, inevitably, limits and identifies the sort of honour that it introduces, but in each honour is more a given of the play than a source of the tragic conflict. This tendency is apparent in *King Lear*, where honour is but one of the seminal ideas out of which Shakespeare created Lear's moral redemption, and his tragedy.

Notes to Chapter 7

[1] See above, p. 16.

[2] Harold Skulsky, in 'King Lear and the Meaning of Chaos', *Shakespeare Quarterly*, XVII (1966), 3–17, advances a similar argument. Glancing at the Trojan council scene in *Troilus and Cressida* for an example, Skulsky probably overstates his case by arguing that 'the scholastic–Aristotelian formula

of the good as the natural, the byword of Anglican humanism, says precisely nothing' (p. 5), but his ensuing discussion of the problems of value in *King Lear* provides a persuasive corrective to the influential reading Robert Heilman, *This Great Stage* (Baton Rouge, 1948), has given the play. 'I should like to suggest', Skulsky remarks, 'that in *King Lear* Shakespeare calmly searches the chaos that Ulysses has glanced at with a shudder'. The play causes us in imagination to 'abolish all mere insignia of justice, human dignity, and love ... and then [to] see whether the supposedly intrinsic values persist' (p. 5). Of the chaos represented in the scenes on the heath, Skulsky remarks that 'as an exterior weather' that chaos has allowed Lear 'to isolate the human root of justice. It has made it impossible for him to fall back on mere labels of dignity and right ...' (p. 11).

[3] Fulke Greville, *Alaham*, Second Chorus, ll. 9–12, in *Poems and Dramas of Fulke Greville* ... , ed. Geoffrey Bullough (New York, 1945), Vol. II. All references to the play are to this edition.

[4] Joan Rees, *Fulke Greville, Lord Brooke, 1554–1628 A Critical Biography* (Berkeley and Los Angeles, 1971), p. 156, apparently believes that the Euill Spirits are merely the group of Furies, i.e. Malice, Craft, and Pride, answering Corrupt Reason with a single voice, a reading which overlooks several details. The heading of the Chorus lists 'Euill Spirits' as a separate character (indeed the 1633 edition of Greville's *Workes* has 'Euill Spirit'. See Bullough, p. 257.); Corrupt Reason refers to the others collectively as 'Furies', (l. 64), rather than evil spirits; the pattern of the Chorus is hierarchical, and it would betray that pattern to reintroduce the lower stages; most tellingly, Craft, Malice, and Pride do not share the positive power for evil which the Euill Spirits claim. That is the whole point.

[5] Ivor Morris, 'The Tragic Vision of Fulke Greville', *Shakespeare Survey*, XIV (1961), 69, recognizes the general similarity between ll. 135–8, quoted here, and some Shakespearian themes by asking, 'How much of Shakespearian tragedy, one might wonder, lives in those lines?'

[6] The animal imagery of the play, as has been widely remarked, also serves to define these characters as bestial and ferocious. Kenneth Muir, in the introduction to the Arden edition of *King Lear* (New York, 1964), provides a brief summary of critical explanations of the animal imagery (pp. lx–lxi).

[7] Castiglione's *Courtier* explicitly argues that a courtier properly gains honour by advising his prince of the virtuous course even if opposition to the prince is thereby necessary. See above, p. 17.

[8] A variety of sources make it clear that the number and quality of one's retinue were widely understood as marks of honour. Holinshed's account, for instance, has Cordelia provide Lear, in France, with money 'to reteine a certein number of seruants that might attende upon him in honorable wise, as apperteined to the estate which he had borne. ...' Cited in Heilman, p. 316. Watson, pp. 154–5, cites evidence of the general attitude and, pp. 197,

424–8, describes Lear's knights as a matter of honour. He is concerned to demonstrate, in opposition to 'the Puritan assumptions of the last three hundred years which [have turned] topsy-turvy our critical interpretations of fundamental ethical issues in Shakespeare's plays' (p. 424), that Goneril's reduction of the King's train would have been considered 'malicious' by a Jacobean audience. He draws no conclusions about the place Lear's honourable retinue occupies in the structure of the play.

[9] That weeping was womanish and therefore dishonourable for a man is another commonplace of Renaissance speculations on honour. Compare Macduff's response to the news of the death of his wife and child, and see Watson, pp. 247–9.

[10] Heilman, for instance, sees Lear's evaluation of 'need' as a comment on the condition of man. He believes the play approves the sort of honour of which the knights are a symbol. 'For the real significance of Lear's followers is this: they are not a literal 'need' but a symbol of something that he as an aged king has earned, and, beyond that, of the gratuity in excess of need, the dignity, the honor, which distinguish human kind from the animal' (p. 108).

[11] There are some similarities in diction between Greville's Chorus and this act. 'Mans skinne', Greville's Evil Spirits say, 'was then his silke', and the statement, 'the worlds wild fruit [was man's] food' expresses the same idea that Edgar's list of 'mice and rats, and such small deer' does. Echoes of other works have been noted (see the note to the passage in the Arden edition for a summary), but, however intriguing the similarities with Greville's play might be, particularly in light of the generally discounted legend that Greville was Shakespeare's and Jonson's master, the fact is that there is no concrete evidence that Shakespeare read *Alaham*. It is not, however, particularly surprising that two, thoughtful contemporaries concerned with more or less the same set of ideas should come to similar judgments in their separate plays. Greville's play sheds light on *Lear* precisely because both his own talent and the requirements of French Senecanism, which the Countess of Pembroke sponsored in England and according to which Greville's two extant plays are formed, produced plays more explicitly philosophical and speculative than any of Shakespeare's.

[12] N. to V.iii.24.

[13] The possibility that *Macbeth* may have preceded *King Lear* is of no particular concern here, for what little indication there is of a distinct chronological pattern in Shakespeare's use of the ideas of honour suggests that it is after *Othello* that he generally makes a different kind of use of the ideas. The tendency to use the idea as one of the givens of a play may be connected with the tendency C. L. Barber sees in the changing meaning of the word as it was used on the stage. 'From the time of Beaumont and Fletcher, honour became one of the absolutes of the drama', Barber asserts (*Honor in the English Drama*, pp. 13–14).

Index

GEORGE ALLEN & UNWIN LTD

Head Office:
40 Museum Street, London WC1
Telephone: 01–405 8577

Sales, Distribution and Accounts Departments:
Park Lane, Hemel Hempstead, Hertfordshire
Telephone: 0442 3244

Argentina: Rodriguez Pena 1653–11B, Buenos Aires
Australia: Cnr. Bridge Road and Jersey Street, Hornsby, N.S.W. 2077
Canada: 2330 Midland Avenue, Agincourt, Ontario
Greece: 7 Stadiou Street, Athens 125
India: 103/5 Fort Street, Bombay 1
285J Bepin Behari Ganguli Street, Calcutta 12
2/18 Mount Road, Madras 2
4/21–22B Asaf Ali Road, New Delhi 1
Japan: 29/13 Hongo 5 Chome, Bunkyo, Tokyo 113
Kenya: P.O. Box 30583, Nairobi
Lebanon: Deeb Building, Jeanne d'Arc Street, Beirut
Mexico: Serapio Rendon 125, Mexico 4, D.F.
New Zealand: 46 Lake Road, Northcote, Auckland 9
Nigeria: P.O. Box 62, Ibadan
Pakistan: Karachi Chambers, McLeod Road, Karachi 2
22 Falettis' Hotel, Egerton Road, Lahore
Philippines: 3 Malaming Street, U.P. Village, Quezon City, D-505
Singapore: 248c/1 Orchard Road, Singapore 9
South Africa: P.O. Box 23134, Joubert Park, Johannesburg
West Indies: Rockley New Road, St. Lawrence 4, Barbados